# *FORWARD PASSES*

## AN ADULT COMEDY

## BRIAN S. WHITELAW

# *Jasper Publishing*

Moulton Park Business Centre, Redhouse Road,
Northampton NN3 6AQ
Tel: 01604 497703 Fax: 01604 497689
jasperpublishing@ukbusiness.com

### *Jasper Publishing*
Moulton Park Business Centre, Redhouse Road,
Northampton NN3 6AQ
Tel: 01604 497703 Fax: 01604 497689

## ISBN 1 904416 03 9

**British Library Cataloguing-in-Publication Data.**
**A catalogue record for this book is available from**
**The British Library.**

# FORWARD PASSES

## CHARACTERS
in order of appearance

**Gary Jenkins** 38
**Hazel Jenkins** 34
**Babs** 40
**Clive** 50
**Sue** 30
**Dan** 40
**Sam** 24

The action takes place in the living room of the Jenkins' suburban home.

ACT 1 8 pm on a Friday evening in late September.
ACT 2 Ten minutes later.

Time: the present.

## DEDICATION

To Ruth, Bridgette and Diane with love.

## FIRST PRODUCTION

FORWARD PASSES was first performed by MLADS at Moulsham Lodge Community Centre, Chelmsford, Essex in June 1994. It was directed by the author with the following cast:

Gary - Daniel Curley
Hazel - Diane Purkiss
Babs - Liz Curley
Clive - Derrick Payne
Sue - Paulette Harris
Dan - Len Robson
Sam - Jenny Teanby

## AUTHOR'S NOTE

This play was written for a typical amateur dramatic group and with a cast of 3M and 4F and a modern set it should be relatively straightforward to stage. There are also few props and minimum requirements of lighting and effects. In the first production a number of lines were changed to suit the characteristics of those cast. However, Dan ought to be bigger than Clive who in turn is bigger than Gary. Hazel and Babs should bear a resemblance, as should Clive and Gary from the rear! Some of the more risque lines were omitted from the first production, or changed to suit it. Permission is given for such minor alterations to suit your needs. The reference to 'Rory Underwood' may become dated and can be changed to any new rugby star, thus allowing the play to stay up to date.

# *FORWARD PASSES*

## ACT 1

*The sitting room of a suburban bungalow. 8. 00 p. m. on a Friday evening in late September.*

*The room is furnished for the most part in modern furniture about 7 years old. Upstage there is a Welsh dresser beside a dining table which has a large hatch above it. Centre right is a sofabed, with small tables either side of it, angled to face the television down right. Downstage left is a desk with papers etc. and a waste paper basket. Between the chair and the sofabed is a beanbag. Other furniture consists of dining chairs, drinks table and bookcase. Doors upstage right lead to the bathroom, stage right to the master bedroom, and stage left to the kitchen and spare bedroom. The room is very tidy except for Gary's cast-off clothes and briefcase downstage centre, by the front door, which is imagined, leading into the auditorium. Beside the imaginary door is a telephone table, partly to give the cast a focus for its opening. Steps lead down from the stage into the "garden" where there are a wheely bin, milk bottle container and garden bench. In front of the sofabed is a soft rug and around the room are pictures, pot plants, books, videos, a rugby trophy, drama group photos etc. There could be a radiator here and there. (See plan).*

*As the curtain rises, Gary is seen sitting at the table upstage centre, finishing off some fish and chips from papers on his plate and engrossed in a rugby video on television which is audible. He is 38, with signs of middle aged spread and hair loss. He is dressed in white shirt - undone with one sleeve rolled up - and the trousers of a suit. His jacket and tie have been thrown on the sofabed and chair. The table holds cans, glasses, cruets and sauce bottles. A kettle begins to whistle and is turned off.*

*After a moment or two, Hazel will enter from the kitchen. She wears an attractive sweater and skirt or dress.*

**HAZEL** *(off)* Tea or coffee Gary?
**GARY** What?
**HAZEL** *(looking through hatch)* I said, tea or coffee?
**GARY** *(distracted)* Yes please.
**HAZEL** Well, which?
**GARY** Oh, er, coffee then.

*A pause . He finishes his last chips with his fingers.*

I always save my biggest one for last!

**HAZEL** *(off)* What are you talking about?

**GARY** *(raising his voice and speaking through a full mouth)* Chips! I said, when we have fish and chips I always save my biggest chip for last.

**HAZEL** *(head in hatch)* Don't talk with your mouth full. I thought you were being crude again.

**GARY** Crude? Me, crude? Saucy perhaps ... *(holding sauce bottle)* but not crude. *(continues to watch the video)*

**HAZEL** *(enters with two mugs)* As soon as I go into the kitchen you switch on the TV. What are you watching now?

**GARY** England versus Australia.

**HAZEL** Thought it was Brookside.

**GARY** This is less predictable.

**HAZEL** But you've seen that one before?

**GARY** That's what I mean!

**HAZEL** Well, give it a break so we can have a chat. *(sits at table)*

**GARY** *(reluctantly getting up to switch off the TV set)* Oh all right! What do you want to talk about?

**HAZEL** I don't know, just talk. We don't do much of it these days.

**GARY** You're dead right there!

**HAZEL** I meant we don't seem to talk much!

**GARY** I'll start. You answer this deeply philosophical question - it's your starter for ten - why do we always have fried fish and chips on a Friday? Is is because (a) it's Friday so they fry, (b) they fry because it's Friday (c) there's nothing to eat in the house or (d) your father had an affair with a mermaid?

**HAZEL** You know perfectly well. When I've been working all week I don't feel like cooking, and secondly, it's fairly cheap and we can't save money to start a family by living expensively. If we really want to save money, we must...

**GARY** *(taking his tea and moving down right to sofabed)* All right Hazel love I know. *(he's heard this before)* Tell me darling, IF we do start a family, and you have to stop work, and we have to buy all those baby things - I'm not saying yes you understand - well would I still be allowed my Friday night out with the lads? *(sits)*

**HAZEL** Yes, always assuming I still get money before my solo scrummage with the Saturday shopping crowds. And BEFORE you go please. Can't have you wasting it all on booze. *(comes downstage with her tea to sit on arm of sofabed)*

**GARY** It isn't wasting it! A night out with the lads, free of feminine interruption, is what a chap needs on a weekly basis. When I was playing rugby every week, we had a great time afterwards! *(breaks into song)* "There was a monk of great renown!"

**HAZEL** Gary!

**GARY** "There was a monk o great renown!"

**HAZEL** I know it!

**GARY** "There was a monk o great renown!"

**HAZEL** Punchline.

**GARY** "Who sold his wife for half a crown!" *(laughs)* I haven't heard that one for ages!

**HAZEL** I can't say I'm sorry. You don't sing songs like that in The Queen's Arms do you?

**GARY** I wouldn't be singing anything if I was lying in the queen's arms! *(laughs)* No, it's not like a rugby crowd in there. Mind you, they've recently started this karaoke lark.

**HAZEL** So, the shopping money?

**GARY** No sooner said than done my Hazelnut. *(reaches into his jacket and passes to her 3 small bundle of notes)* The one thing I always do to please you on a Friday is to fill up with petrol and fill in with cash. Can't go without the shopping.

**HAZEL** To please me? I like that. You can't go without your beer!

**GARY** Oh yes I can! ... Or I could if I wanted to.

**HAZEL** Well, don't get too drunk will you. You've got work to do tomorrow.

**GARY** But I've been working all week!

**HAZEL** For the last I don't know how many Saturdays you said you'd move that lorry load of hard core from the side way. Whether a front porch ever gets built on this house or not, it. would a great help if we could at least put the bin out of sight!

**GARY** All right love.

**HAZEL** Seriously Gary, ever since we moved here, we thought a porch would be useful for coats and the phone, not to mention the inconvenience of the front door opening right into the living room.

**GARY** Yes I know. I'll see what I can do tomorrow.

**HAZEL** You've been saying that all summer. I've been thinking lately that. the only hard core you're interested in is what you can get on video from your mates!

**GARY** *(surprised)* How do you know about those?

**HAZEL** It's me that keeps this place tidy and I'm not blind! *(points to video tapes)* I don't think the tape you've hidden up there called "Swedish Indoor Games" is anything to do with Scandinavian rugby competitions!

**GARY** *(excited)* Do you want to watch it with me?

**HAZEL** No I don't! But thanks for this (indicating the money) I'll put it safe. *(gets up and goes towards kitchen)* You clear the table remember!

**GARY** Chores, chores, chores. *(gets up wearily)*

**HAZEL** You can talk! What chores?

**GARY** Thanks, I'll have a pint of bitter!

*Hazel groans and exits. He moves to the table passing the rugby picture on the bathroom door and bows. He then gathers up the mass of paper into a rugby ball. He breaks into a commentator's voice.*

**GARY** And Rory Underwood collects the pass from Carling deep inside the England half and makes his way up field, avoids one tackle, then another, pushes Campesi aside as if he was made of paper, and touches down for what has to be the winning try!

*After circuiting the room he dives on to the beanbag and places the ball of paper into the waste paper basket. Hazel enters with an empty milk bottle.*

**HAZEL** *(amused by his antics)* Look at you! When are you going to grow up?
**GARY** *(lying, exhausted)* I might, one of these days!
**HAZEL** *(putting the bottle "out")* I would prefer that you still played real rugby and got rid of some weight. You're beginning to get a beer belly. *(puts her foot on him)* The only exercise you get is what your right arm does when it lifts a dart or a beer glass!
**GARY** *(approaching her on all fours like a randy dog and she backs away until she sits on the sofabed)* Well, just occasionally I get to exercise another part of my anatomy!
**HAZEL** Down boy, not now you don't! There's a time and place!
**GARY** It won't take long!
**HAZEL** *(sitting)* Yes, that's the trouble! Remember I'm going out too this evening. Don't look so surprised! I told you on Tuesday.
**GARY** I thought you were looking a bit smart.! Where are you off to then? Some hen party? *(clucks as he climbs up beside her)*
**HAZEL** You must have been half asleep as usual. *(patiently)* When I came in after drama on Tuesday, I told you that we were having an extra rehearsal for the new play and tonight was the only night we could make.
**GARY** You and your amateur dramatics! I don't know what you see in it! A lot of hysterical middle-aged women prancing about all over the place living out their fantasies! *(suggestively)* You could live some of yours out with me.
**HAZEL** I don't get your kind of fantasies!
**GARY** (in American accent) Sorry to hear that honey - 'cause you know, life could be even more fantastic!
**HAZEL** *(appreciating his talent)* You should come to the drama club!
**GARY** Not me... I don't make a fool of myself in public...
**HAZEL** But you never even come to see the productions.
**GARY** I don't like to see you making a fool of yourself!
**HAZEL** Well you should take up an active hobby Gary. There are lots of interesting classes starting just now,
**GARY** I tried didn't I? When was it, two years ago? First I tried yoga and tied myself in knots! Then cookery - I ought to be able to cook standing on my head - but the trouble was that every couple of weeks I had to be away overnight and missed it. And then I didn't know what recipe we were doing and what ingredients to take. Talk about a recipe for disaster! *(pause)* So you'll be late in tonight as well?
**HAZEL** Not as late as your usual wee small hours! I expect we'll go for a drink afterwards, but I'm tired, it's been a long week.
**GARY** How is life among the tiny tots?
**HAZEL** Oh don't ask.
**GARY** Depressing isn't it? What a world to bring kids into! Perhaps that's why they call it a depression cos it makes everyone so bloody depressed! It's the same all over the place. Travelling around trying to sell stuff to people who don't want to buy and couldn't even if they did. Do you know what happened today?
**HAZEL** Of course! *(laughs)* No, how could I? You haven't told me!

**GARY** I went to Hodgekinsons in Birmingham to get their monthly order and show them the new range and the bloody place was all boarded up! Deserted it was. Eventually I found a watchman and asked where everyone was. I thought the firm had re-located. Not a bit. He said "Last week the management just announced the firm had gone to the wall. Closed down. Every man jack of the work force has been laid off!" So bang goes that client! *(sighs)* I just hope I don't get laid off! *(snuggles up to her)* I wouldn't mind getting laid though.

**HAZEL** *(serious, but amused too)* Gary, you never take life seriously for long do you? Get off down to the pub! *(exits to the master bedroom to fetch her handbag)*

**GARY** *(getting up and stretching)* All right little woman. I know when I'm not wanted.

*He sees the waste paper basket, goes over, picks it up, opens the front door and places it in the space. He takes three steps backwards from it and two steps to the side, and it just about to kick it into the 'garden' when Hazel enters and sees what he's up to.*

**HAZEL** Hold it there Rory Underwood! If you think I'm going to clean up a mess of uneaten fish and chips you're mistaken! *(puts her bag on the sofabed, picks up the basket, empties it into the wheely bin, then closes the door)*

**GARY** What is this life if full of care we have no time to ... kick the air!

**HAZEL** *(threatening to hit him with the empty basket)* Don't stand there dreaming! Go and change!

**GARY** What into? A handsome prince?

**HAZEL** I think I prefer you as a frog. Go on!

*Gary jumps to attention, clicks heels and gives an exaggerated Nazi salute.*

**GARY** Yavol! Your vish ist mein command mein fuhrer! *(exit to bedroom)*

**HAZEL** *(after him)* I don't keep this place tidy for you to mess it up. *(replacing basket by the desk)* And take the rest of your clothes! *(throws into him his jacket and tie)* I wish you wouldn't. leave them lying about! *(pause)* You and your rugby! People must think you're mad supporting England with a name like Gareth Jenkins! *(sits on sofabed and looks into her handbag)*

**GARY** *(entering in light blue jeans, carrying trainers, and pulling on an old rugby shirt)* My father may have been Welsh, but I'm born and bred in England and I'm proud of it.

**HAZEL** First you talk with your mouth full, and then with a that old shirt over your head! What ARE you saying?

**GARY** *(his head coming through)* I said I'm English and proud of it!

**HAZEL** When you have a son, at least he'll have English parentage! If you were fit you'd be able to teach him to play.

**GARY** What if it's a daughter? Girls play rugby now too you know. When the big ones run with the ball you can't tell which it is! *(laughs)* Now if they introduced mixed rugby I might be tempted to take it up again!

**HAZEL** Get away with you! Even when you were fit, you didn't run fast enough to catch cold, never mind a girl! Proper little confirmed bachelor you were when I met you.

**GARY** You're right there. I was never very fast, either on my feet or in the company of women. Much more interested in other pursuits. An easy catch for a vulture like you! If I did get fit again, do you think I could escape?

**HAZEL** Huh! You wouldn't want to. Here you live like a king!

**GARY** Then perhaps I'd better get into The Queen's Arms!

*The telephone rings and Hazel goes to answer it, Gary being busy tying up his trainers on the chair by the TV.*

**HAZEL** Hello? ... Hold on. *(puts receiver down and sits)* It's Dave.

**GARY** What does he want? *(crosses to phone)* Hi Dave ... Yes I won't be long ... Yes, course I do... Really? Well, that's interesting. Hold everything till I get there ... I said - watch my Lips - oh you can't, can you - I said hold on till I get there OK ... Soon ... Cheers! *(hangs up)*

**HAZEL** What did he want?

**GARY** Who, Dave?

**HAZEL** No, the queen! Won't Dave be at the pub?

**GARY** *(hesitantly)* Yes ... but they may be one short in the darts team and he wanted to check I'd be there.

**HAZEL** Do you ever miss?

**GARY** The dart board yes, but not the pub if I can help it!

**HAZEL** And so that you don't strain your throwing arm by swinging it as you walk, you'll be taking the car?

**GARY** Of course. When do I get to use my company perk for pleasure?

**HAZEL** Well, if you drink too much, leave it there and walk home. You'll be out of a job if you lose your license, never mind the danger of running down any of the neighbourhood cats.

**GARY** There's always the wheelbarrow.

**HAZEL** Oh don't get into that state again, Gary. I don't know what the neighbours must've thought.

**GARY** Have we got any neighbours then? I never see them.

**HAZEL** Go on, off with you! *(pushes him towards door)*

**GARY** *(seeing his bag)* Oh I nearly forgot. *(opens his bag and produces a rather crushed small bunch of flowers)* For the lady in my life!

**HAZEL** Well, I suppose it's the thought that counts. *(pecks him on the cheek)* Enjoy your evening.

**GARY** *(opening front door)* I will my lovely. You too. Don't you go overacting. *(kisses her and wants a longer clinch, but she pushes him out)* Unless it's with me! Give us a wave ... oh yes what's this? *(waves his arm)*

**HAZEL** A wave?

**GARY** And this? *(waves his fingers by his shoulder)*

**HAZEL** Tell me!

**GARY** A microwave! Here, and this? *(shakes his head)*

**HAZEL** Well?
**GARY** A brainwave!
**HAZEL** *(laughing)* See you later, aggravater!

*Gary sings the rugby world cup anthem as he walks down the path. From the rear of the hall we hear a gate close.*

*Hazel has watched him go for a moment then closes the door. She takes a new cassette tape from her handbag and plays it. It's a topical romantic number. She hums as she takes the flowers and places them at the back of the table. She then goes into spare room and re-enters with a package of nappies and bottle of baby's milk which she also places on the table. She sniffs the room, takes some things from the table into the kitchen and returns with a fresh air spray which she liberally uses round the room. Towards the end of Hazel's activity, Babs approaches up the garden. She is about 40, with similar build and hair colouring to Hazel. She is a nosy chatterbox but a competent baby-sitter. She is dressed in a summer frock with a cardigan. She reaches up and rings the bell. Hazel comes back from the kitchen and opens the door.*

**BABS** Mrs Jenkins?
**HAZEL** You must be Babs. Do come in.
**BABS** *(entering)* Thank you dear.
**HAZEL** I hope you didn't mind me ringing you at such short notice.
**BABS** Oh don't worry about that! Only too pleased to help out. Mind you I don't usually go out on a Friday. I'm a bit tired by then. But Madge said it was a kind of emergency.
**HAZEL** Yes, well it's good of you to come.
**BABS** It's a pleasure dear. As I say, it's nice to help someone out. And I don't mind getting out of my house I can tell you. it's no fun being stuck in there all day. Get a bit of peace and quiet.
**HAZEL** Have you come far?
**BABS** Oh I only live two streets from here ... no distance really. I've often seen these old bungalows at the end of the long front gardens and wondered what they were like inside. *(looks round)* You keep it very tidy. It's not easy with a baby around, I know.
**HAZEL** My husband untidies and I tidy!
**BABS** I know just what you mean. *(sniffs)* Fish and chips supper tonight Mrs Jenkins?
**HAZEL** Er, yes ... and do call me Hazel. Here, have a seat.

*Babs has circuited the room and now sits and makes herself comfortable on the sofabed. Hazel goes to stop the tape and switch off the player, She then wanders the room during the dialogue with Babs drawing the curtains, completing her tidying and inspection. Babs stretches and yawns.*

**BABS** That's a nice name! Can't be shortened can it? You'd never guess my full name! *(before Hazel has a chance to)* No, it's not Barbara, it's Barbarella! When I was a girl, there was a sexy film with Jane Fonda in it. Wish I had her figure! She's amazing, looking like that at her age!

**HAZEL** My husband sometimes calls me Hazelnut.

**BABS** Oh I get it! He sounds a laugh. What's he like?

**HAZEL** Oh, Gary's all right, good natured but a bit scatterbrain. Behaves like a child.

**BABS** Men never grow up dear. Take my Trevor now. He' s forty-three but he still plays with train sets. Can you believe it? He says he buys them for the kids but they've grown out of them.

**HAZEL** How old are they?

**BABS** Twelve and ten. Into pop music, comics and all those noisy video games.

**HAZEL** Gary watches videos a lot. On that shelf up there he's got I don't how many recordings of rugby matches. It beats me that he can watch them over and over again. *(puts Gary's video away)*

**BABS** Takes all sorts. Don't mind my asking dear, but what does he do for a living?

**HAZEL** He's a travelling salesman. Hard work these days. The only time he gets to relax is Friday evenings when he's a member of what I call the BBC - the Boys' Boozing Club! *(draws right 'curtain')*

**BABS** Likes his drink does he?

**HAZEL** Oh I think he goes mainly for the company. A hangover from his rugby days. He doesn't usually drink too much.

**BABS** Where does he go then?

**HAZEL** The Queen's Arms. *(crosses to draw left 'curtain')*

**BABS** Oh I know, in the High Street. I went there when I was a teenager to meet the boys. One coke lasted me all evening! Lived here long?

**HAZEL** About seven years, since we got married.

**BABS** And before that? Do you come from round these parts?

**HAZEL** No, we came here because Gary wanted to be near the motorway, for his work you know, and the housing was a bit cheaper. *(picks up and takes out to master bedroom Gary's case)*

**BABS** But you like your house don't you?

**HAZEL** Yes, it's all right. It's old and solid and could do with a porch but it's all we could afford at the time.

**BABS** I think you did well.

**HAZEL** It only has the two bedrooms and I'd like something a bit bigger but I don't suppose we'll move with money being so tight.

**BABS** You'll be saving up for your second then?

**HAZEL** What second home? *(pushing tablewear through the hatch)*

**BABS** Baby! You told me on the phone there was just the one. Is it a boy or girl?

**HAZEL** A boy.

**BABS** That's nice. It's good to have a boy first. You be clever, have a girl next and make up a set. They'll be good company for each other when they're older. I don't mean the age of my two at the moment... always squabbling they are. I mean later when they go out to discos and such. And how old is he?

**HAZEL** Thirty-eight. *(goes into kitchen)*

**BABS** I don't mean your husband dear!

**HAZEL** Oh, the baby! ... Six months? *(through hatch while removing things)*

**BABS** You don't sound very sure!

**HAZEL** Yes, he'll be about six months.

**BABS** Any teeth yet?

**HAZEL** Not as far as I know.

**BABS** And what do you call the little man?

**HAZEL** Well Gareth is his full name, but everyone calls him Gary.

**BABS** No I mean the baby dear.

**HAZEL** Er ... He's called Peter.

**BABS** I expect he'll get Pete. Is he a good baby?

**HAZEL** Oh yes, never cries at all. (closes hatch and comes back)

**BABS** Babies are so different aren't they. You must know, working at the nursery unit. Even in the same family, kids can be quite different, with one as good as gold and the brother or sister a little terror. Yes, you're lucky with Pete! My two were both howlers. No sooner had I got one shut up when the other would start. Sometimes one would start the other off. There were times when we slept them one at each end of the house! Where does Pete sleep?

**HAZEL** *(winces)* There in the spare room. *(points)*

**BABS** Not spare any longer! You should get some of those nice little name plates, you know Baby's Room or Peter's Place. When he grows up I expect he'll call it Pete's Pit! *(laughs)*

**HAZEL** Well it's a good size second bedroom. Apart from the cot, there's a bed and cupboards, so we just haven't got round to calling it anything else. The baby's fast asleep, and I'll only be about an hour so there shouldn't be any need for you to go in to him. *(applies lipstick at the bathroom mirror)*

**BABS** And are there any other occupants?

**HAZEL** What do you mean, lodgers?

**BABS** Pets dear.

**HAZEL** No, why?

**BABS** Well I once got a terrible fright. I was babysitting for another neighbour, Mrs Jones it was, perhaps you know her, lives next to the doctor's house?

*Hazel shakes her head.*

Anyway, I was watching the telly and I fell into a deep sleep - I get very tired of an evening - when the next I knew something heavy landed in my lap! It was a bloody great ginger cat - pardon my French - God it scared the life out of me I can tell you! *(laughs, a pause)* And where are you off to then Hazel?

**HAZEL** I'm in a drama club and there's a short rehearsal ...

**BABS** I haven't done any of that since I was at school 25 years ago. All girls secondary school I was at and when we did drama I usually got a boy's part. *(laughs)* Nowadays I have enough drama at home to keep me busy. What play are you doing?

**HAZEL** It's a thriller called "On the Run". *(takes her script from the shelf, and taps it on her hand)*

**BABS** Not keen on thrillers myself. Keep me awake. Give me a nice drama with a bit of romance thrown in. And where do you do your drama?

**HAZEL** Oh, it's not far, the Baptist Hall. *(replaces the script)*

**BABS** Oh yes I know. You get off now then Hazel and don't worry.

**HAZEL** And you make yourself comfortable Babs. The kitchen's there if you want a coffee, or there's something stronger it you prefer. and there's a remote control if you want to watch television.

**BABS** Oh I won't watch anything. It might put me to sleep. Perhaps I'll read. I've got a nice Mills and Boon.

**HAZEL** Yes, well, I'll fetch my jacket. *(goes into master bedroom)*

**BABS** Don't worry yourself about me. I'm just glad of a little peace and quiet away from trainsets, video noises and pop music. *(yawns)*

**HAZEL** *(re-entering wearing light jacket)* Good, I'll be off then. *(moves to front door and turns)* Oh, what about payment?

**BABS** *(getting up)* Never mind that just now. We can sort it out later. You get off and rehearse.

**HAZEL** Bye then.

**BABS** Bye, no need to hurry back!

*Hazel closes the door and goes down the path to click the gate. On Hazel's exit from the house, Babs goes straight into the master bedroom for a moment, re-enters without her cardigan, heads for the bathroom, adjusts her hair in the mirror, comes back to the front door, opens it and loudly whispers...*

**BABS** Clive!

*Clive, aged about 50, seated in the audience, has seen Hazel go and crept up to hide behind the wheely bin. He wears some light blue slacks, shirt with cravat, V-necked naval sweater and white shoes. Babs comes down the steps, calls again, and he grabs her from behind. She yells.*

**BABS** Oh, you frightened the life out of me! Come in quickly!

**CLIVE** Try stopping me! *(enters and Babs closes the door)* It was getting a bit chilly out there! And uncomfortable in those rose bushes!

**BABS** Been there long have you?

**CLIVE** Only a few minutes. You did say eight fifteen didn't you?

**BABS** That's right.

**CLIVE** And you know I never come late. *(sniffs)* You been eating chips?

**BABS** No. How are you? *(moves towards him and he pecks her cheek)*

**CLIVE** In need of a drink. Where's the booze?

**BABS** Over there I think. *(indicating)*

*Clive makes for the drinks as Babs begins another tour of inspection.*

**CLIVE** First class! I very nearly called out to the housewife! In the dying light she looked a bit like you!

**BABS** She's a nice lady, called Hazel. Husband's Gary.

**CLIVE** I expect you kept her back with your chattering!

**BABS** Well you've got to be sociable, haven't you? You can't walk into people's houses and kick them out. Whatever would they think?

**CLIVE** Cinzano all right for you?

**BABS** Lovely. *(wanders off round the room looking at ornaments etc and sees photographs above desk)* Bit of an actress is our Hazel. That's where she's off to. Seems to be quite a star, judging by all these photos.

**CLIVE** *(bringing drink to her and looking at photo she holds)* She looks very fetching in that costume! I'd help her out of it. Now there's an idea! Join the drama club and get a job as wardrobe master!

**BABS** Oh Clive! Would you want me as wardrobe mistress?

**CLIVE** You can leave out the wardrobe! Cheers! *(drinks a sip of whisky, pinches/smacks her bottom and crosses to sit on the sofabed)*

**BABS** Ouch! Can't you wait for a bit? *(drinks deep)*

**CLIVE** That's exactly what I'll do! Long enough to get my bearings.

**BABS** Here, you've made this drink strong!

**CLIVE** Couldn't see any lemonade. I must say this is a surprise Babs. There I was this afternoon, checking the wages bill and wondering what the weekend had in store for me, when you ring up with the time and place. First class!

**BABS** I very nearly didn't as it's Friday but I thought you'd like it! Hazel didn't give me much notice.

**CLIVE** I don't need much! Usually got time for you my dear. You just have to say where and when.

**BABS** *(having finished her snoop, comes to sit beside him)* Well it was your idea Clive, you clever boy. Do some baby-sitting you said, and I'll come and help you pass the time! *(snuggles up)*

**CLIVE** *(pride in his craft)* Well it's a perfect arrangement isn't it? Your husband has his hands full with your terrors and of course my wife doesn't give a damn where I am. We meet at a different place each time so no-one knows where we are, or what we're up to.

**BABS** And we've seen some places haven't we Clive? I'll never forget that time we met in Grange Park! That great four-poster was very romantic wasn't it?

**CLIVE** I should say so! My only regret was not having any ropes! Now when I was in the navy...

**BABS** You told me that at the time and I said you could forget your sailor's knots!

**CLIVE** Well it's nice to add a bit of excitement. Why don't you find a place with a waterbed!

**BABS** That might be all right for you - I can't swim! *(giggles)*

**CLIVE** I'd lifesave you! Now there's something I'd like to try!

**BABS** Whatever do you mean?

**CLIVE** I'll show you later. *(laughs lecherously)* I sometimes think you're more interested in the house than the bed. You never waste any time snooping around the place.

**BABS** That's not fair! It's just interesting exploring other people's houses and seeing all their bits and pieces. You can learn a lot about people by looking round. You're only interested in one thing!

**CLIVE** Don't say you're not interested?

**BABS** Well I could certainly do with a lie down. *(yawns)* I don't know if meeting here tonight was a good idea.

**CLIVE** Now you tell me! I'll go if you like! *(moves to get up)*

**BABS** Oh no, Clive! I didn't mean it! *(pulls him down)*

*The telephone on the table by the front door rings. They just listen to it ring two or three times without moving and then carry on talking.*

**CLIVE** Trevor doesn't know you're here of course?

**BABS** Oh no, you said we shouldn't give him any idea.

**CLIVE** Or get involved with the family here. Stick to the system. *(lights a cigarette as they wait for the phone to stop ringing)*

**BABS** You shouldn't smoke in here.

**CLIVE** You can say you had a cigarette can't you.

**BABS** (yawns) How are the kids?

**CLIVE** Oh we've just heard that the lass got through the cadet training school exams she took in the summer so now she's fully fledged as they say. And the lad seems to have settled into college, or he should have, judging by the bills I've had to pay, hall fees, books, etc. etc. Thank God he'll cost me less on haircuts and school uniforms. The jeans he's got now should last the duration! I still wish he'd followed me into the navy though.

**BABS** But it must be nice to have them both off your hands. Can't wait till my two follow suit. My whole life seems to revolve around shopping, cooking, cleaning, washing, and as for ironing, I've got piles!

**CLIVE** Sorry to hear that Babs.

**BABS** You are a one! Hazel keeps this place tidy though doesn't she? Just wait till the baby starts moving around! It'll be chaos then.

**CLIVE** Where is the baby?

**BABS** In there. Do you know, Hazel wasn't sure how old he is! Strange that. Perhaps I should check he's all right. *(goes to door)*

**CLIVE** *(as she reaches the door)* No, don't do that! Let sleeping dogs lie! If you wake him now God knows if he'll get to sleep again!

**BABS** *(returning to sofabed, she stands behind Clive to give him a neck massage)* I suppose you're right. Here, remember when that little brat screamed the place down?

**CLIVE** Will I ever forget it!

**BABS** It's a chance we have to take with the small ones. At least I don't sit now with older children.

**CLIVE** Thank God for that!

**BABS** I couldn't help it! I got the ages of the kids wrong that was all.

**CLIVE** And left me waiting outside for half an hour in the cold till you got a chance to come and tell me to go home! Third class that was!

**BABS** Well, they were running all over the place! I had to get them settled down to watch a cartoon before I could risk leaving them. And they didn't even get to bed before their parents came home!

**CLIVE** Here, talking of babies, this woman goes to dentist and she says, "I'm so worried about this treatment, I'd rather be having another baby," and he says, "Well would you make up your mind before I adjust the seat!" *(laughs loud)*

**BABS** *(laughs a little as she sits again)* Oh, before I forget, next Tuesday's off.

**CLIVE** Next Tuesday?

**BABS** You remember. I was asked to babysit at that place round in Jubilee Street, well, it's off.

**CLIVE** Jubilee Street's been off for years! You mean that place with the twin beds and no central heating?

**BABS** That's the one. She rang up last night and said they weren't going out after all. Somebody ill or something.

**CLIVE** I can't say I'm sorry. I nearly caught my death of cold!

*Babs yawns again.*

You very tired?

**BABS** A bit. Don't know why I get so tired of an evening these days. Perhaps it's my age.

**CLIVE** You're as young as the woman you feel! *(he does)*

**BABS** Be patient! We'll go in a minute. *(yawns again)* Oh. dear ... that neat Cinzano hasn't exactly woken me up!

**CLIVE** Maybe I'll keep you awake!

**BABS** Yes, you' re never too tired are you? Here, except that time when we both fell asleep ... do you remember?

**CLIVE** Lord yes! I should say so! I'd had a particularly hard day. You dropped off and I followed suit. Next thing I knew was that couple standing over us and him asking me who the devil I was! *(laughs)* I turned to you and called you wife and you thought it was Trevor!

**BABS** And I asked you to bring me a cup of tea! I bet our faces were red! *(laughs)*

**CLIVE** Well, somehow we got out of it.

**BABS** They haven't asked me back though!

*They laugh. A moment.*

**CLIVE** We should stick to that story again if we need to. I'm Trevor and I've managed to dump the kids with neighbours so that I could come and ... I don't know ... give you some family news or something ... maybe somebody's died.

**BABS** Yes, all right.

**CLIVE** How is Trevor by the way?

**BABS** Oh, same as usual. Dead boring. He only gets excited when he gets a new engine.

**CLIVE** His own one is a bit clapped out isn't it!

**BABS** Either that or he just doesn't find me interesting any more.

**CLIVE** I suppose it's the same with Marjorie. Twenty years ago, she couldn't get my socks off quick enough. Now I've got time to knit myself a pair.

**BABS** Well you were hardly ever there were you? Always sailing off to some distant parts.

**CLIVE** Our parts couldn't be more distant now!

**BABS** Well, I'm glad! I don't want to share you. *(yawns and rises)* Oh dear, I'm ready for a lie down. You coming? *(slowly exits)*

**CLIVE** I'll just finish my Players. *(takes his glass to top up, stubs out his cigarette)* Right then! Duty calls! Action stations! Stand by to receive boarders! *(He "pipes" himself and follows her with his drink into the master bedroom, dimming lights by wallswitch)*

*Shortly after the bedroom door is closed, the gate and voices are heard at the back of the hall. Gary and the giggling barmaid Sue approach, Sue holding on to Gary's arm to stay steady on her high heels. She wears a short summer dress with buttons or zip down the front.*

**GARY** This is the house, up here.

**SUE** Looks a cosy little place. Lights are on. Sure she's out?

**GARY** Yes, now come on! *(He doesn't want them to be seen)*

**SUE** I can't 'urry in these 'eels.

**GARY** I hope the car's safe. I usually bring it up to the gate.

**SUE** Oh you don't 'alf worry. 'Elp! *(stumbles and grabs him and then sits on the garden bench)* I think I've gone and laddered me stockings!

**GARY** You've had a drink already tonight haven't you?

**SUE** Just a little one at me local, The Cock Inn - DON'T say it! I needed some courage to chat you up outside the Queens.

**GARY** You didn't let me get near the bar! Dave told me you were lying in wait for me you little vixen! Well this is it. Come on! *(opens door with key and shows her in)*

**SUE** *(circuiting the sofabed)* Well, I didn't fancy working in the pub tonight - I fancied meeting you instead!

**GARY** *(closes the door and she throws her arms around his neck)* Hold your horses, give me a chance! You are an impatient little girl aren't you?

**SUE** Oh, I don't know. I've waited me chance for months, watching you in the bar every Friday, but if you're not interested, I'll go! *(lets him go and turns away)*

**GARY** Oh, no, don't do that... we're here now. Of course I'm interested. It's just a bit of a surprise that's all. I'm not used to this kind of thing. And to come here of all places... *(moves downstage left to check curtains are drawn)*

**SUE** Oh don't panic Gary. When I suggested it, you said your sister 'ad gone out. If she comes back, well., what's it to 'er?

**GARY** It's just that I've never brought a girl back here before.

**SUE** What never?

**GARY** No, honestly.

**SUE** You 'ave been out with girls before 'aven't you? *(moving to him)*

**GARY** *(with nonchalance)* Oh yes, course I have.

**SUE** Well, if your sister comes back early, I'm sure you'll think of something.

**GARY** Yeah, like what?

**SUE** *(crossing stage right)* Well... let me see now... you could say that I took sick in the pub... and you took pity on me... and brought me 'ome to your 'ouse ... and put me to bed!

**GARY** And that I got in beside you just in case you fell out. Some story! She's bound to believe that!

**SUE** I reckon you need a drink to give YOU courage.

**GARY** Good idea, what would you like? *(heads for the drinks table turning lights up on his way)*

**SUE** Vodka please, and 'ave something for yourself. That sounds funny! In the pub I'm used to asking you what you'd like!

**GARY** You mean when I give you an order for drinks?

**SUE** Yes, nothin' else worst luck! *(sniffs)* 'Ere, you been eatin' chips?

**GARY** Course not, place always smells like this.

**SUE** *(at master bedroom door)* What's in 'ere?

**GARY** That's the master bedroom

**SUE** Come on then, let's explore it!

**GARY** Later, have a drink first.

*Sue pinches him, peeks inside the bathroom, says, "Nice big bath" and moves on to reach the dining table where she sees nappies and bottle.*

**SUE** Is your sister married?

**GARY** *(his back is to her)* No, what makes you ask that?

**SUE** 'As she gotta baby then?

**GARY** Not as far as I know!

**SUE** So is this your nightcap?

*He turns to see her holding bottle.*

And are these for you to wear in bed? *(holds up the nappies and finds this hysterical)*

**GARY** Quiet Sue, you'll burst a blood vessel! I don't know what they're doing there!

**SUE** Pull the other one! *(wanders towards the photos)*

**GARY** *(perplexed)* Honestly, Hazel does strange things sometimes.

**SUE** Does she? I do strange things too!

**GARY** I bet you do!

**SUE** No, I ain't talking about sex! Not this time. Do you believe in your stars, the supernatural, witches an' that?

**GARY** Can't say as I do really.

**SUE** I do. I reckon that me and you was fated to meet one day. Last Sunday, me stars said that later in the week I might meet someone who could be good for me!

**GARY** And I believe that when I went out this evening, and Hazel went off to her rehearsal, her good fairy flew through the letter box with that bloody great bundle of nappies as a sign of her impending motherhood!

**SUE** I believe you, but thousands wouldn't! I'm a very trusting person I am.

**GARY** *(taking a last puzzled glance at the baby things and then following her with the drinks)* Well you can trust me!

**SUE** Pity! *(giggle)* Is this your sister in all them play photos? To be or not to be that is the question! *(swings her arms and nearly swipes Gary)* What's she like?

**GARY** Er yes, that's Hazel. Here's your vodka.

**SUE** Cheers! *(sips)* She never comes down the pub.

**GARY** She tried it once when we first moved here, but doesn't really like pubs. Let's sit down shall we? *(tries to steer her from wedding picture but is too late)*

**SUE** 'Ere, what's this weddin' picture? That's you, and 'er! You and 'Azel... I can see the likeness ... you didn't tell me you was married.

**GARY** Well, you didn't ask! I'm sorry Sue. But now you know I'm married I don't suppose that you ...

**SUE** Oh that's all right. Don't make no difference to me!

**GARY** *(surprised)* Doesn't it

**SUE** I been out with married blokes before. On the 'ole I find they're more considerate. I think I prefer older men anyway. They're a bit more patient an' all.

**GARY** I see, well, I think you'll have to be patient with me.

**SUE** You never answered me question. What's 'azel like?

**GARY** *(crossing in front of her to the photograph)* Well, you can see can't you? *(picks up the photo)*

**SUE** I mean to live with. Is she more of a sister, than a wife?

**GARY** Oh, she's all right. Trouble is, she's getting a bit broody. Keeps talking about starting a family. *(places photo face down)* She's sure but I'm not.

**SUE** Not what?

**GARY** I'm not sure I'm ready for it.

**SUE** *(saucily)* I am!

**GARY** I mean ready to start a family!

**SUE** Judging by all them nappies, I reckon she's got one on the way now! Probably 'ave it tomorrow! *(laughs)*

**GARY** I think I'd know if she was! I do know she's ready for the mysteries of motherhood.

**SUE** 'Ark at you! The mysteries of muvver'ood! I ain't ready for 'em. Not my scene. I like to be free. Do what I wanna do. *(crosses to the sofabed and sits at TV end)* Come over 'ere! *(pats the seat beside her and Gary slowly follows)*

**SUE** Is Hazel G. I. B? *(leans towards him)*

**GARY** Eh? What do you mean?

**SUE** Is she G. I. B, good in bed?

**GARY** Er... oh yes ... excellent! As soon as the light is put out, she goes straight off to sleep. *(pause)* She never, ever snores, and doesn't wake up until the alarm goes off!

**SUE** You nutter! Have you had a lot of experience?

**GARY** At what?

**SUE** Seducing girls.

**GARY** Oh yes, tons. Well no, I can't say as I have really. Not had much chance I suppose.

**SUE** I like that! You've been giving me the eye in the pub for months you 'ave! I can tell just by the way you ask me for pints! Go on, you just ain't 'ad the courage to ask me out, 'ave you? Some men are all talk and no trousers. Perhaps you're no talk and just trousers! *(grabs his trousers)*

**GARY** Perhaps I'm neither! *(struggling with his drink to hold her off)* Hold on Sue!

**SUE** I'm trying to!

**GARY** Everything will be all right in the end!

**SUE** That's what I'm trying to discover!

**GARY** *(getting up and moving downstage left)* Don't rush me like that! God what have I done!

**SUE** What was that"?

**GARY** I said ... what have I done ... leaving my car round the corner.

**SUE** You ARE uptight aren't you? Relax, and let it all 'ang out!

**GARY** Perhaps that's why I'm uptight!

**SUE** 'Ere Gary, are you sure you're not a dad?

**GARY** Well of course I am!

**SUE** You do know what to do, don't you? *(lies back seductively)*

**GARY** Yes, and we will ... if I can ... if we can. I mean if we want to, it's just that being here, in my home, with a strange woman ...

**SUE** Oh I like that! I aint strange!

**GARY** I don't mean strange, I mean different, new.

**SUE** Don't you fancy me then?

**GARY** Course I do. But maybe we shouldn't have come here. *(pause)* Tell you what - how about a video? *(moves behind sofabed to the shelves)*

**SUE** You mean you need something to get you in the mood? Is it naughty?

**GARY** Would you like that?

**SUE** Not 'alf!

**GARY** Er, well, no, nothing like that. I just thought you might like to see a film or something.

**SUE** What film do you mean then?

**GARY** Well, the other evening I recorded "Casablanca".

**SUE** That goes on for bleedin' hours!

**GARY** *(Bogart's voice)* Here's looking at you kid! The night is young sister!

**SUE** But we ain't got all night! I wish we 'ad!

**GARY** So, no film then?

**SUE** I never brought you back 'ere to see no film!

**GARY** Well, do you play any sport'?

**SUE** Only the indoor variety.

**GARY** Well, er, how about a game of indoor rugby?

**SUE** Wot?

**GARY** You know, throw a ball about for a bit. *(grabs the bundle of nappies)* Here, catch. *(throws it and then goes to a cupboard for his children's rugby ball)*

**SUE** Gary you ain't 'alf daft! *(stands, catches nappies and puts them behind the sofabed)* Look if I don't turn you on, why don't you put on some music? Hmm? Something smoochy to get you going? I can tell you're a bit shy. *(sits again)*

**GARY** *(passing his ball from hand to hand and moving downstage left)* Well, I'll try, but I'm not very sure that it'll work ... it's funny what turns different people on isn't it? You may find this hard to believe Sue, but playing rugby always used to put me in the mood, you know, an hour or two after the match. The experience of scrumming down, feeling the other guys' thighs...

**SUE** Don't tell me that you're ...

**GARY** No, nothing like that! It's just that the physicality of the game is rather arousing and ...

**SUE** Do what?

**GARY** Oh, nothing.

**SUE** You're interested in men's bodies are you?

**GARY** No, of course not! *(puts the ball in the basket)*

**SUE** Well that's a relief! Not that I've got anything against that sort of bloke ... it takes all sorts. *(pause)* 'Ow about that music then?

**GARY** *(crossing front stage)* OK, do you like Dire Straits?

**SUE** Yeah, "Brothers in Arms" I suppose! Find something relaxing.

**GARY** *(at the cassette recorder)* Let's see ... what's this"? *(plays the cassette Hazel was playing)* I don't remember this.

**SUE** It's great! Now turn it down a bit and come over here. *(pats the seat beside her)*

**GARY** *(in a Noel Coward voice)* Be gentle with me my darling!

**SUE** You are frustrating!

**GARY** A bit frustrated perhaps, but not frustrating surely? You don't feel guilty, being with a married man? *(sits)*

**SUE** I'm a liberated woman I am. Men chat me up all the time, married men too, just trying to get me into bed. Just because I make the first move don't mean I'm common.

**GARY** No, I didn't mean that Sue.

**SUE** It's just that I fancy your body something rotten! *(grabs him)*

**GARY** *(struggling)* Tell you what!

**SUE** NOW what?

**GARY** This music's a bit mournful! Let's have a dance!

*He gets up before she can prevent him and stops the music. Sue looks disgusted.*

I know, let's do a haka! *(looks for the tape)*

**SUE** Do what?

**GARY** A Maori haka, listen! *(acts it out a few moments)*

**SUE** You're mad! *(turns the tape off)*

**GARY** Well shall we dance? Come on, let's have a bit of exercise!

**SUE** It aint THAT kind of exercise I want!

**GARY** But you're a good dancer! I've seen you in the pub!

**SUE** But I didn't come 'ere to dance! I can do that any time!

**GARY** Perhaps I should take you back to the Queens then.

**SUE** But we just got 'ere!

**GARY** Tell you what.

**SUE** *(with despair)* What is it this time?

**GARY** What would you say to a nibble?

**SUE** *(saucily)* Yes please!

**GARY** No, I mean something to eat. You know crisps, twiglets, nuts ...

**SUE** Looks like the only nuts I'll be getting tonight!

**GARY** That's if I can find any. *(heads for the kitchen)* I don't know where things are kept. There might not be anything cos Hazel goes shopping on a Saturday you see.

*Immediately he is in the kitchen, Sue shrugs her shoulders, gets up, and goes into the bathroom, closing the door. From the master bedroom Clive appears, wearing just trousers held up by gaudy braces. Hearing Gary rabbit on in the kitchen, he crosses until he is beside the hatch.*

**GARY** *(continuing)* No there are none there, *(door slams)* or there. *(again)* God knows where she keeps them. Ah, here we are. What would you like? Cheese and Onion? Prawn Cocktail? Salt and Vinegar? Plain? Sausage and Bacon. Marshmallow and Peppermint?

*Each time he announces a flavour, he hurls the bag through the hatch and they pass narrowly in front of Clive's face. He sticks his head through.*

**GARY** Are you getting enough? *(doubletakes Clive)* Sue? What the ... Talk about the supernatural!

**CLIVE** What are you up to in there? Come out will you?

**GARY** *(emerging gingerly from kitchen, limply holding a rolling pin)* What's happening? Who are you? Did Sue let you in? Where is she? Well are you going to tell me or ... *(raises pin threateningly)*

*Gary swings at Clive who disarms him with a simple unarmed combat technique and twists his arm behind his back. They face the audience.*

**CLIVE** There's no need to be violent! YOU do the talking! Who are you? What are you doing here?

**GARY** Nothing, er, fetching crisps, er I'm not doing anything.

**CLIVE** No? Well who are you? Come on, out with it!

**GARY** I'm, er, just visiting!

**CLIVE** Breaking in eh?

**GARY** No, I'm visiting ... oh, to meet the owners ... I'm the ... er, brother of the owner ... the twin brother!

**CLIVE** And what are you doing here?

**GARY** I've just come round to borrow some crisps! And, oh, to have my arm broken ... Oh, I do that often. I've got a key you see. I live just round the corner. Are you alone?

**CLIVE** Never mind that. *(lets Gary go)* Here put this dangerous weapon away before you hurt yourself. *(thrusts the rolling pin down the front of Gary's trousers)*

*Gary heads for the kitchen. Clive comes to pick up the crisp packets, ending downstage left. Sue enters behind him and takes up a pose against the door frame. She has shed her dress hoping that this will do the trick. She holds the pose for a moment, and then, seeing "Gary", half-naked and on his knees, she advances and she puts her arms round him from behind.*

**SUE** Well, hello there Mr Chippendale!

**CLIVE** *(drops crisps)* Babs? *(turns and rises and she jumps back in shock. He wastes no time)* My word! First class! I say! *(steps towards her)*

**SUE** Get away! Who are you? Are you a burglar?

**CLIVE** If you have something worth stealing!

**SUE** *(retreating towards TV, round the sofabed and the room until she is in front of the sofabed)* 'elp! 'elp!

**GARY** *(enters from kitchen and sees Sue under attack)* Leave her alone! *(playing the hero, he runs at Clive, who is moving downstage centre and brings him down on the rug with a rugby tackle aimed at the knees)*

**CLIVE** Get off me you swine!

**GARY** Quick Sue, help me, come and sit on him!

**SUE** Oooh Er, Where do you want me to sit? On his ...

**GARY** On his body!

**CLIVE** I think you've broken my knee!

**GARY** I'm glad to hear it.!

*Sue sits on his torso.*

Now you tell me what YOU'RE doing here?

**CLIVE** I'd be glad to if I could breathe!

**GARY** Come on, out with it!

**CLIVE** I will if you get her off!

**GARY** Ease up Sue.

*She does.*

**CLIVE** *(rolling on to side facing audience)* Thank you my dear. Under normal circumstances I'd be very happy to have you sit on me.

**SUE** Oh you're too kind!

**GARY** Enough of that! Now speak up mate. Who are you?

**CLIVE** *(having now had time to think)* If you must know... I'm a member of the drama club.

**GARY** Oh yes?

**CLIVE** I was told the rehearsal was being held here!

**SUE** Why are you 'alf naked then?

**CLIVE** Well isn't that bloody obvious? ... It's a dress rehearsal. I was ... getting into my costume!

**SUE** Gettin' out of it more like!

**GARY** Who invited you here?

**CLIVE** Er, well, Hazel did of course.

**GARY** I don't know whether to believe you or not. Sue, I think he might be a burglar or some kind of pervert. We should tie his hands behind his back.

**SUE** What with?

**GARY** I don't know ... this is a crisis ... let's have your bra.

**SUE** You gotta be jokin'. It's a new one on tonight.

**GARY** Sue, listen to me. This is no time for modesty.

**SUE** Well, as long as it's in a good cause! (*she is about to unhook her bra, when, from the master bedroom ...*)

**BABS** *(off)* Where are you?

**GARY** *(looking up)* Now, who the devil can that be?

**BABS** *(off)* Are you there dear?

**GARY** *(getting up and going to bedroom)* This isn't happening!

**SUE** *(retreating towards kitchen)* Don't leave me with 'im!

**GARY** Oh, you'll be all right Sue! *(enters bedroom and immediately re-enters and comes to address Clive)* Who the blazes is that woman hiding in bed?

**CLIVE** Take it easy old chap.

**SUE** I suppose it's another member of the drama club!

**CLIVE** Yes, that's it, she's another member of the drama club!

**GARY** And I suppose that in this dramatic performance she doesn't get to wear a costume at all!

**CLIVE** Yes, you see that play is em ... about Lady Godiva and we've reached the part where ...

*Babs enters from the master bedroom wearing Hazel's dressing gown and goes straight into the bathroom. Gary turns just in time to see her.*

**GARY** Hazel! *(to Clive)* What have you been rehearsing with my wife?

**CLIVE** Don't you mean your brother's wife?

**GARY** Yes, er, of course that's what I mean. *(exchanges a look with Sue)*

**CLIVE** Well it isn't.

**GARY** Isn't what, my wife or my brother's wife?

**CLIVE** Neither!

**SUE** What are you two goin' on about?

**GARY** Leave this to me Sue! *(goes over to the bathroom door and hammers on it)* Hazel, are you in there? Answer me!

**BABS** Who's that?

**GARY** Come out here!

**CLIVE** *(moving on to the sofabed)* I'm trying to tell you it isn't Hazel!

**SUE** *(to Clive)* Well who is it then ...

**GARY** Hold it Sue. *(tries handle)* She's locked herself in! Hazel, if you're in there ...

**CLIVE** Of course she's in there. Let me handle this.

**GARY** She might have climbed out through the window! She could be in the back garden by now, trying to escape over the fence.

**CLIVE** Well, yes that is a point, but pretty unlikely I should say.

**SUE** Oh yes? Why's that then?

**CLIVE** Well, she's probably only wearing that dressing gown.

**SUE** That'd be awkward to climb in, wouldn't it? I mean the window aint very big and she ...

**GARY** Look, shut up you two! *(at door)* You in there!

**BABS** What do you want?

**GARY** Stop whatever it is you're doing and come out!

**BABS** I can't stop!.. And I'm not Hazel!

**CLIVE** What did I tell you.

**GARY** Well then, Lady Godiva, let your hair down and come out!

**SUE** That's good, that is, "let yer 'air down!"

**BABS** Where's Clive?

**GARY** Who's Clive?

**CLIVE** I'm Clive!

**SUE** 'E's Clive!

**GARY** *(coming to Clive)* Right, CLIVE. Get her out of there. *(goes down stage right)*

**CLIVE** Well I offered to but you told me to ...

**GARY** Get her out!

*Toilet flushes.*

**CLIVE** Righto. *(getting up and hobbling across to the bathroom. He taps the door)* Babs? This is Clive. You can come out. It's OK.

**GARY** Babs? Babs? *(crosses stage to join Sue)*

**SUE** I reckon it must be Babs!

**BABS** Is it safe?

**CLIVE** Yes, it's quite safe. No one will harm you.

**BABS** *(unlocks the door and enters gingerly)* What's going on Clive? Who are these people?

**CLIVE** *(guiding her to TV end of sofabed)* It's all right now.

**BABS** I must have fallen asleep when I heard all this thumping and fighting and banging! I needed to spend a penny so I thought I'd make a bolt for it.

**SUE** But there is a bolt for it!

**CLIVE** *(with a look of disdain at Sue)* Yes, I know, but it's all right. I got disturbed too! It was some damned strange chanting that roused me! *(from behind sofabed)* Look, you two, this is a bit awkward isn't it? Meeting up like this. Why don't we all sit down and try to get things shipshape in a civilised manner

**SUE** It's you MEN what's being uncivilised!

**GARY** You're sure there's no one else lurking in some cupboard.

**CLIVE** As sure as I can be. Come on, what d' you say?

**GARY** Well it can' t do any harm. Might clear the air a bit. All right then. Sit down Sue.

*Clive makes to sit beside Babs but Sue gets there first. He then brings up the chair from beside the TV and places it near to Babs. Gary puts the crisps through the hatch and drops into his favourite spot on the beanbag.*

**BABS** *(as Sue sits beside her)* Hello dear, so you're Sue. How are you?

**SUE** Mustn't grumble. 'Ows yourself?

**BABS** My head's as heavy as lead. I feel someone's hit me.

**SUE** I got aspirins in me bag. D'you want some?

**BABS** Are you sure it's no trouble?

**SUE** No trouble at all love, just you...

**CLIVE** *(impatiently)* All right district nurse! That can wait a minute.

**SUE** But she's got an 'eavy 'ead! It's all right for you.

**BABS** I'll have an aspirin presently dear. Better let him have his say or we won't hear the end of it. Go on Clive.

**CLIVE** Thank you very much! *(clears his voice)* Now, as I see it, we four belong elsewhere. I mean, we don't any of us live here. So... er perhaps we should explain our presence. *(points to Gary)* Maybe you'd like to start?

**GARY** Oh, who me? Yes, well, as I said just now, I'm the brother, the er twin brother, of Gareth Jenkins, the man who owns this house.

*Sue looks at Gary and sniggers.*

I just popped round here with my girlfriend here, Sue, to see how things were - I often do you see, I have a key - and er, I was just getting some...

**SUE** Nibbles.

**GARY** Yes, I was getting something for us to eat, while Sue was...

**SUE** 'Aving a wash I was.

**GARY** Yes, 'aving, er having a wash she was, when you surprised me.

**CLIVE** Well, don't blame me old chap. I thought you were acting a bit suspiciously.

**GARY** How do you mean?

**CLIVE** Not many people I know mutter to themselves while they hurl packets of crisps through a kitchen hatch!

**BABS** Oh I don't know. Stranger things happen at sea!

**CLIVE** Well, yes, I should say so!

**GARY** But what are you two doing here, as if I can't guess!

**SUE** I think I can guess! They was doin' what we should've been doin'... in the bedroom making mad, passionate I...

**GARY** Yes thanks Sue. We don't need a graphic description! But are you really members of the drama club? Did Hazel say you could use the house for your... hanky panky?

**BABS** Well, you see, it was like this...

**CLIVE** *(puts his hand on Babs' arm to stop her giving his game away)* 'Course she did! We thought that naturally she would have cleared it with her husband.

**SUE** Oh, it don't really matter Gary! *(giving Gary's game away)*

**CLIVE** Gary? Gary? As I thought. You're no twin brother! You live here!

**BABS** I thought he did too. He looks just like the man in the rugby photo over there.

**GARY** Yes, well, all right I am, yes and er, Hazel is my wife and Sue here...

**CLIVE** Sue here is your bit on the side.

**SUE** Not yet I ain't. I ain't had much chance!

**GARY** Well, now you see how it is, Sue thought,, well we thought that the house was empty and came in to sort of, sort of...

**SUE** 'Ave it off!

**GARY** Delicately put. *(changes the subject)* Well, now that we've all been introduced, sorted a few things out, I could use a drink.

**CLIVE** First class idea! I'll fetch our glasses. Mine's a big one.

*Sue exchanges a look with Babs as Clive goes to the bedroom leaving the door open. Gary heads for drinks table.*

**BABS** I don't want to be awkward or a stick in the mud, or anything, but I think I'd prefer a nice cup of tea. It might wake me up.

**SUE** I'll make you one Babs and I'll get those aspirins. *(heads for the bathroom first to get her dress which she brings outside the bathroom door to put on)*

**BABS** It's all that Cinzano, and this mixup, making my head spin.

**SUE** 'Ere Babs, are you really doing Lady Godiva?

**BABS** Bless you no dear. I'm not very good at acting. That's Clive for you. The last thing I acted in was...

**CLIVE** *(entering wearing sweater again, carrying glasses)* Don't you believe her Sue, she's very good! *(with relish)* The role I like her in best is when she's a schoolgirl with pigtails and gymslip. Takes me right back to boarding school days!

**BABS** *(waving Clive to her as she gets up)* Clive, don't you think we ought to explain properly?

**CLIVE** Leave things as they are, Babs, bit of a laugh this! *(aloud)* Now you two girls run along and have a nice chat and a cup of tea and we'll rehearse more later! *(nudging her knowingly)*

*Sue, having done up her dress, picks up her handbag and goes into the kitchen. Clive ushers Babs in to join her. Sue looks through the hatch.*

**SUE** 'Ere's the weather forecast for tomorrow. Dark clouds are 'overin' on the 'orizon!

**GARY** Thank God for that, I've been praying for rain.

**SUE** There'll be rain an' all!

**GARY** Then I might get out of some digging I'm supposed to do!

**SUE** You two be'ave yourselves in there! *(closes the hatch and opens it again)* And no playin' rugby! *(closes the hatch)*

**CLIVE** I wouldn't mind playing rugby with her! Bit of all right is Sue!

*Gary hands him his drink.*

Thanks. Cheers! I must say Gary, you had me going there for a minute! Brother of the owner, the twin brother as well! First class!

*He sits on the sofabed and puts his leg up just as Gary is about to sit. Gary heads for the beanbag.*

**GARY** Well, I didn't know who you were. You could have knocked me down with a feather when you said you were friends of Hazel. She's probably told you all about us.

**CLIVE** Not a lot actually! I can't say I know Hazel particularly well, But don't you worry old man, mum's the word, never fear. I won't spill the beans.

**GARY** *(with relief)* That's good of you Clive.

**CLIVE** We men have to stick together in situations like this. Isn't that your experience?

**GARY** Well, no. To tell ynu the truth, this is actually the first time I've been tempted to stray from the straight and narrow.

**CLIVE** Really.

**GARY** Don't take much interest in other women. But as you can see, Sue is, well, *very* persuasive.

**CLIVE** I should say so! First class!

**GARY** Her idea to come here when I let slip that the house was empty.

**CLIVE** Mistake that, old boy. Never whatsaname on your own doorstep. That's rule number one. You're almost bound to leave some evidence of occupation.

**GARY** Is that so?

**CLIVE** You'd better believe it. Perfumes are the worst danger. Nasty they are as evidence. Women have noses like bloodhounds.

**GARY** Hazel wouldn't need a nose if she walked in here now! She'd only need her eyes.

**CLIVE** I hear what you're saying.

**GARY** If she found me here with Sue, never mind you and Babs, God knows what she'd do!

*They drink a moment.*

**CLIVE** How long you been married?

**GARY** Just over seven years.

**CLIVE** The old itch eh? Never really experienced it myself.

**GARY** No?

**CLIVE** No, my itch, as they call it, started when I was about seventeen and I've been scratching it ever since, thirty odd years!

**GARY** Are you not married then?

**CLIVE** Oh yes! I was in the navy at the time. Getting married was like having a more permanent girl in one particular port if you get my drift. Made long leave a bit more comfortable. And when I came out of the navy, I'd got used to a good deal of variety among the fairer sex, so I just found ways and means of carrying on, carrying on! *(laughs)*

**GARY** You mean you've been having affairs all your married life?

**CLIVE** Well, you can't have them before can you now!

**GARY** Does Hazel know that you and Babs are... you know?

**CLIVE** I shouldn't think so. I'm very careful about. covering my tracks rule number two, always have a good alibi!

**GARY** I've heard that a certain amount of hows-your-father goes on in these amateur dramatic circles.

**CLIVE** Oh, Babs and I like a bit of role play but I wouldn't say that we are typical members of any drama club.

**GARY** No?

**CLIVE** I should say not. Definitely not.

**GARY** Does your wife know about your affairs?

**CLIVE** Oh, I very much doubt it. She might suspect but she can't know.

**GARY** What would you do?

**CLIVE** If she found out you mean? Deny it of course. Lie through my teeth. That's rule number three - never confess to an affair. You've got to be an accomplished liar. Sometimes I tell my missus lies just to keep in practice! So it's something we never talk about. She does her thing and I do mine!

**GARY** And Babs is your latest thing? *(handles his rugby ball)*

**CLIVE** The latest in a very long line old boy. *(drinks with satisfaction)*

**GARY** How long have you been seeing her?

**CLIVE** About nine months. After a while I get a bit bored and feel ready for a change. I think I'm one of those men who were never really cut out for the married life. Travel and variety seem to be in my blood. So every so often I hoist sail as you might say.

**GARY** Why did you get married then?

**CLIVE** Why do any of us do anything? Social pressure I guess. Before I knew where I was I had a regular port of call and two young sprogs to feed. But once a rover, always a rover. *(changing tack)* I haven't seen that Sue of yours before.

**GARY** Oh, she's a barmaid at the Queen's Arms. It seems that tonight she felt like working on me instead of behind the bar!

**CLIVE** I like it!

**GARY** I was very nervous about the whole thing I can tell you! I still am! I like her all right but, I don't want life to get too complicated.

**CLIVE** That's how you strike me! And you've got an honest face! You're not really cut out for running around with the likes of Sue!

**GARY** Is that what you think?

**CLIVE** I certainly do. She's a flighty little number isn't she? I think she needs a more experienced sort of man to keep her under control.

**GARY** Really?

**CLIVE** Oh yes, she's the sort that needs her bottom smacked at regular intervals. Now, if you do decide to stray from the primrose path, you should go for someone a bit quieter and shall we say, discreet. Someone who's not going to open her mouth and put her foot in it! Someone like Babs.

**GARY** You think so?

**CLIVE** I know so. You can't afford to have someone lively like Sue threatening to wreck your marriage. And things change once you're a father too, don't they?

**GARY** Oh yes, and they should! I think a man should take his full share of parenthood once a couple have begun their family. I've never thought it should be left to the woman to do it all.

**CLIVE** That's where we're different old boy. For me a woman's place is in the home and for the man it's out and about, hunting you might say! Once you get tied down domestically, you'll never be able to play the field, Gary, you take my word for it.

**GARY** To be honest, I've never felt inclined to play the field as you put it. Can't say I look much at other women.

**CLIVE** You don't know what you're missing!

**GARY** But as far as Sue's concerned, well, when someone like that makes herself so readily available, it's hard to resist! I mean, she's the sort you can't help noticing, isn't she?

**CLIVE** I should say not. She stands out a mile! Here, talking of pubs and barmaids, this young lad goes up to the bar and asks for 20 fags and a pint of best bitter, and the barmaid says, "How old are you?" and he says, "Fourteen", and she says, "Well you've had it," and he says "Yeah and don't it make you thirsty!" *(laughs)* Then she says, "Are you trying to get me into trouble?" And he says, "One thing at a time, one thing at a time!" *(laughs again)* I wonder what those two are up to out there.

**GARY** Having a little hen party.

**CLIVE** They're very quiet. They might have dozed off. At least Babs might. She could sleep on a sixpence that one.

**GARY** I think I should take Sue home. *(goes to the drinks table)*

**CLIVE** *(with emphasis)* Oh, don't do that old boy! Heavens no! What time is your wife due back?

**GARY** Oh, not for a couple of hours.

**CLIVE** Well then, there's plenty of time yet!

*Sue and Babs enter.*

**CLIVE** Talk of the she devils, here they are! *(stands and takes a few paces towards the kitchen)* What have you two smashing girls been up to then?

**BABS** *(entering holding a coffee mug)* Well, I'm having a black coffee but I still feel a bit woozy Clive. *(heads downstage, turns the desk chair to face the audience and sits)*

**SUE** *(entering just behind Babs)* I need a refill. *(heads for the drinks table and talks quietly to Gary)*

**CLIVE** *(takes look at Sue's rear and follows Babs)* Not feeling too good then old girl?

**BABS** Why did you tell them we were from the drama club? What it they ask us about it?

**CLIVE** Leave it to me. It's only a bit of fun. Can't do any harm.

**BABS** Well, now Gary's here, we can go, can't we?

**CLIVE** Of course we can't! How can we leave here before Gary? What if his wife came back and found him with that little raver?

**BABS** Well, that's his lookout. If he can't handle it...

**CLIVE** Oh, he wants to all right!

**BABS** I still think I should tell them what I'm doing here.

**CLIVE** What for? It's a good laugh putting on an act. We'll tell them if we have to. Just leave it to me.

*Gary goes into the bathroom and Sue approaches Clive and Babs. Clive has sat on the sofabed near Bahs and Sue sits beside him.*

**SUE** *(to Clive)* Well then, hello sailor!

**CLIVE** Who's been talking - as if I can't guess!

**SUE** She told me all about you when we was out in the kitchen.

**CLIVE** Oh Babs likes a good chinwag, don't you love?

**BABS** Well I was only being sociable. And Sue was very kind to me. You can't sit in silence can you?

**CLIVE** Well Babs, YOU certainly don't find it easy.

**BABS** Be a bit more sympathetic Clive. I'm not feeling myself.

**CLIVE** Neither is anyone else! *(laughs and turns to Sue for some appreciation)* She told you all about me then?

**SUE** *(giggles)* Not 'alf sailor boy! Know all about knots do you? Are you into bondage an' that?

**CLIVE** Babs, you shouldn't go about...

**SUE** You men share secrets don't you? I bet you talk about your sex lives all the time!

**CLIVE** And is that what you and Babs spent time in the kitchen doing?

**BABS** We talked about other things as well.

**CLIVE** Like what'?

**SUE** Well, you've got your own business aint you? Got any openings for a promising young girl?

**CLIVE** *(laughs)* That depends on what promises you make!

**BABS** Clive, remember where you are.

**CLIVE** What sort of skills do you have for sale Sue?

**SUE** Well I can do a bit of typing. Me short'ands not much cop, they used to say me long legs would make up for me short 'and!

**CLIVE** Who said that?

**SUE** Blokes in the office where I worked when I left school. They said the only things I was good at filing was me nails! That was a laugh that place, but I didn't stick it for long. I don't like working reg'lar hours. I'm not a nine to five sort of girl. I Like changes. So, what sort of business 'ave you got then?

**CLIVE** Oh, buying and selling. Mostly for the building trade. I'm what you call a middle man.

**SUE** Well, some men like legs, some bums, some other bits, so I suppose it's each to 'is own! *(giggles)*

**CLIVE** Oh well, in that line of business I don't confine myself to middles!

**BABS** No he doesn't! You can take my word for it.

**CLIVE** I should say not!

**GARY** *(enters, picks up his drink and comes downstage to stand behind Sue)* Sue, when you're ready I think we should go and rescue my car and I'll take you back to the pub.

**SUE** Why? I'm just beginning to enjoy meself! Any rate I ain't goin' back there tonight. I was gonna say I was sick when I get in there tomorrow.

**GARY** We could go to some other pub.

**SUE** No we couldn't! It might get back to the Queen's if I was seen. I don't wanna lose this job.

**CLIVE** How long since you've had it?

**SUE** Don't be so personal! *(giggles)*

**GARY** He means the job Sue!

**SUE** Oh, about a year I suppose.

*The phone rings and Gary goes to answer it, but as he is about to pick up the receiver, he stops.*

**GARY** Hold on a minute, I can't answer that! I'm not supposed to be here! Clive you take it. *(turns to go and sit on the chair by the television)* Don't say I'm here. Take a message.

**CLIVE** Er, well, perhaps... I don't think I... Babs, you take it!

**BABS** *(with emphasis)* Leave it to me you said!

**CLIVE** *(seeing no way out, picks up the receiver)* Hello?... Yes?... Who is it?... Yes, as a matter of fact he does... No, I'm afraid he's tied up at the moment... *(laughs)* Who shall I say's calling?... What name is it?... Hello? *(then to the others)* She's hung up! *(puts the receiver down and returns to the sofabed)*

**GARY** What was all that about?

**CLIVE** Well, you heard what I said. This woman wanted to know if a Mr Gareth Jenkins lived here and was he in. When I said yes and asked who was calling, she just hung up.

**SUE** Was she breathin' 'eavy?

**BABS** Women don't make that sort of phone call.

**CLIVE** I wouldn't mind if they did. You know, these days you can call up these special numbers and get a woman to talk dirty!

**BABS** How do you know that?

**SUE** How do you reckon 'e knows? 'E rings 'em up!

**CLIVE** *(indignant)* Oh no I don't. You read advertisements about them in the papers. There are big ones in the tabloids.

**SUE** Yeah, I seen 'em, on page three! *(giggles)*

*A moment. Gary has been puzzling over the phone call.*

**GARY** *(getting up to pace)* What sort of voice did she have Clive?

**CLIVE** Pardon?

**GARY** What kind of voice did she have? Young? Old? Any accent?

**CLIVE** Well, youngish but very ordinary really.

**SUE** I bet you got lots of women chasing after you Gary. Go on confess! Which one do you think it was?

**GARY** I've no idea... I mean I don't know who it was... and I haven't got lots of women chasing after me!

**CLIVE** Chance would be a fine thing!

**SUE** *(to Clive)* You're the sort that does the chasin' you are.

**GARY** Do you think it was someone from the drama club?

**CLIVE** I don't think so though the voice was a bit familiar.

**GARY** Not Hazel then? You both know her don't you?

**BABS** Well, I wouldn't say that...

**CLIVE** Only at the drama club! People there tend not to mix socially at other times. You know you just go there, get on stage, act, and get off.

**SUE** Like you got off with Babs!

**CLIVE** I mean that you just go home afterwards, well usually. You never go there yourself Gary?

**GARY** No, doesn't interest me.

**CLIVE** *(relieved)* No, I thought I hadn't seen you down there.

*Babs registers disgust.*

**GARY** Is Hazel a good actress?

**CLIVE** I should say so! First class!

**GARY** And did she suggest that you two came here, or did you ask?

**CLIVE** Well... she invited us. Isn't that right Babs?

**BAGS** Yes, yes she did invite ME as a matter of fact.

**SUE** And you wanted to come 'ere for the same reason as us!

**BABS** In a manner of speaking, only...

**CLIVE** Quite! We were just you might say, relaxing, when I heard this yelling blasting through the wall and...

**SUE** Playtime was over!

**CLIVE** Well, maybe it was only interrupted! I mean we could sit here and chat, or perhaps we could, you know, continue where we left off. What do you think Gary?

**GARY** *(flippantly)* We've got four for cards.

**SUE** You gotta be jokin'... unless it's strip poker!

**CLIVE** Yes! That's where she strips and you p ...

**BABS** Clive!! I'm not taking part in any communal strip, thank you very much!

**CLIVE** Typical! Well, look, we're all people of the world, broad-minded and that. Couldn't we just take a berth each and continue?

**SUE** Oh yes, why not? We wouldn't get in each other's way!

**CLIVE** And even if we did, I wouldn't mind it a bit!

**BABS** Clive, we are not going to take part in any orgies tonight so you can put that idea out of your head!

**CLIVE** Oh all right. Well, Gary?

**GARY** *(sitting)* I don't know...

**SUE** You don't 'ave to sound so keen!

**CLIVE** Come on Gary, look, you have your bedroom, and Babs and I will put down this convertable, what do you say? This is a bed isn't it?

**GARY** Yes it is, but... well, you have the bedroom, you've started so you might as well finish.

**BABS** I've had enough of this conversation! *(heads for the master bedroom)*

**CLIVE** But it's your house after all!

**GARY** That's as may be but you're the guests and if Hazel said that...

**SUE** For Gawd's sake, you two! It don't matter! Stop goin' on about it!

**CLIVE** Well just as you like old boy... we'll take the bedroom and you stay in here... unless you'd like to swap half way through? Swap beds or...

**SUE** 'ow would you know when you was 'alf way through? Ring a bleedin' bell?

**CLIVE** Right, see you later then. *(stands)* You know, you're not going to believe this you two, but Babs thinks she's only come here as a baby-sitter! *(laughs and goes into the bedroom, closing the door)*

**GARY** *(laughing)* He's a lad that Clive! You never know what lie he's going to come out with next! First class!

*A pause as Gary and Sue look at each other. Sue motions Gary to her with an index finger and Gary gets up to top up his drink or exit to the bathroom depending on how long it takes Sue, once Gary has moved, to put down the sofabed. Gary turns, or returns, and is surprised how much Sue means business. She advances to him and he backs away until he falls on the bed.*

**SUE** *(toppling on him)* Come 'ere, lover boy. *(embraces and kisses him passionately. He comes up for air)* Oh, just one last thing, Gary. I forgot. 'Ave you got a wotsit?

**GARY** A wotsit? Oh you mean a... thingummy! Oh god! *(goes over to the master bedroom and knocks quietly on the door)*

**SUE** They'll never 'ear that! Shout out! *(takes off her dress)*

**GARY** Ah yes, er ... Hold everything in there!

**SUE** They probably are by now!

**CLIVE** *(off)* Yes, what is it?

**GARY** I want to come in a minute!

**SUE** *(aside)* You're not the only one mate!

**CLIVE** All right then, enter!

*Gary enters the master bedroom and emerges with a rolled up blanket and holding up a small packet in his teeth. He throws the blanket like a rugby ball and dims the lights a little. Nervously he removes his shirt and trousers and joins Sue. We hear a few giggles etc as they snuggle down under the blanket. Then a baby cry is heard from the spare bedroom.*

**GARY** *(sitting up)* Did you hear that?
**SUE** 'Ear what? Get down 'ere!

*He is about to when another louder cry is heard. Both sit up and look at each other and then towards the spare bedroom. A third even louder cry brings the head and shoulders of Clive round the door of the master bedroom. A fourth earsplitting yell is heard and Babs enters, wearing a dressing gown, or underwear, or, for the very brave, nothing, (or holding the dressing gown in front of her to cover her nudity) and hurries with some difficulty straight across the room and over the sofabed into the spare bedroom. The others gaze after her as the curtain falls/blackout.*

# ACT 2

*It is ten minutes later. Babs is revealed seated at the desk feeding the "baby" from the bottle and Sue is watching the procedure. Clive, smoking, reclines on the sotabed which is still extended. Gary, with the toy rugby ball, is thoughtfully pacing the room. They are all partially dressed. The lights are up.*

**GARY** Well OK, I have to believe you Babs. You MUST be the babysitter. But what's he doing here? *(indicating Clive)*

**BABS** I invited him here to keep me company.

**CLIVE** Chance would be a fine thing!

**GARY** So the pair of you have nothing to do with the drama club?

**SUE** I reckon they've caused enough drama 'ere.

**GARY** You can say that again Sue.

**SUE** I reckon they've caused enough...

**GARY** Yes all right. Well Clive? What do you have to say? You've been having us on about knowing Hazel.

**CLIVE** Well, yes old boy... no harm meant I'm sure... just a bit of fun!

**BABS** It was his idea Gary. I wanted to tell you the truth.

**CLIVE** He was just as bad! That bit about being his own twin brother!

**GARY** Yes, well, I suppose that's right. But I'd like to know how that baby got here.

**CLIVE** Stork, old man. Ask a silly question.

**GARY** Thanks, I'm not talking biology. So you brought the baby here and when it was asleep you invited Clive in?

**BABS** I didn't bring it here. It was here when I came.

**GARY** What? Then it must have been here when I was. Either that, or Hazel brought it in after I'd left. I didn't see any nappies or stuff here before I went out.

**BABS** Well, I don't know anything about that I'm afraid.

**GARY** When did Hazel contact you?

**BABS** She rang me this morning. She works with a friend of mine.

**GARY** And what did she tell you about this baby?

**BABS** Nothing much. Just that it was about six months old and called Pete. I just assumed it was hers, and of course yours.

**GARY** I think I'd know if I was the father.

**CLIVE** You might. Plenty of men are unaware of the number of kids they father! When people ask me how many children I have, I always say, "Two, as far as I know!" Now when I was in the navy...

**GARY** But I don't go sleeping around like some people I could mention!

*A pause after this outburst.*

**SUE** Cute little thing aint he? Almost cute enough to make me broody.

**GARY** Don't you start!

**SUE** Oh I ain't serious. I got past that stage now. Funny in it, when all me mates was gettin' married and 'aving kids - or 'aving kids and gettin' married - I sometimes felt it'd be nice, you know. But now they're all bogged down with 'em, and 'ardly get out of their 'ouses. Not for me all that 'ousework! Still, you gotta say, Pete 'ere's a sweetie! Look at them little 'ands! *(to Gary)* 'Ere Gary, 'old 'em. *(pulls Gary to the baby and steps back)*

**GARY** *(softening)* Aren't they tiny! But it's his eyes I'm looking at. I can't see any resemblance to Hazel, or anyone else I know.

**CLIVE** How well do you know your milkman?

**BABS** Oh do be helpful Clive.

**CLIVE** I AM being helpful. Many a housewife has got more from her milkman than a pinta milka day!

**GARY** *(moving downstage right)* I don't ever see the milkman. He's come and gone before I'm up. We could have a milkwoman for all I know.

**SUE** *(moving behind Clive to join Gary)* That's a job I wouldn't mind... but only if all the 'ousewives were 'ouse'usbands! *(giggles)*

**CLIVE** You'd never finish your round!

*Laughter from Clive and Sue.*

Here, a husband says to his wife, "Someone told me that our milkman has made love to every woman in this street except one." And she says, "That'll be that stuck-up bitch at No 27!" *(laughs)*

*At this stage Gary and Babs are doing their best to be serious, Clive and Sue seeing the jokes in everything. Clive is trying to impress Sue.*

**BABS** *(after a pause)* Here Sue, do you want to hold Pete?

**SUE** Oh no thanks, I'd probably drop 'im!

**BABS** If it's not your baby Gary, whose is it?

**GARY** Search me.

**SUE** Come 'ere then! *(attempts to search him)*

**GARY** Hold on Sue! I'm trying to be serious!

**SUE** So am I!

**BABS** Perhaps she borrowed it for some reason. Or maybe she decided to baby sit for someone else.

**GARY** *(crossing downstage towards Babs)* But if she did that, she could have rung you up and asked you to go there instead of coming here.

**CLIVE** Don't look for logic where women are concerned old boy. Their brains just don't work the way ours do. What to you and me seems perfectly logical, to them seems natural, if not biological.

**BABS** Pete needs changing. Can somebody fetch the nappies?

*Babs takes the baby to the spare bedroom and Gary puts his toy ball on the table, fetches the nappies and then follows her. Sue moves behind the sofabed and soon sits beside Clive.*

**SUE** That's a job I wouldn't like, changing a baby. You gotta think of the nasty side to 'aving babies as well.

**CLIVE** I should say so. I'll never forget one occasion when my kids were small and I let my missus go out for a bit - God knows why - anyway my three year old daughter was very plump, rolls of Michelin tyres round her. I found her coming out of the toilet saying she'd done her number twos all by herself. Christ, you should have seen the mess! There was sh...

**SUE** Yeah, well spare me the details. I bet you didn't let yerself in for that again!

**CLIVE** I should say not!

**GARY** *(entering)* It's a boy all right! *(sounds proud)*

**SUE** Quite clever aren't you? Able to tell the difference!

**CLIVE** Vive La Difference!

**GARY** Cute little thing!

**CLIVE** Do you mean the baby, or his...

**SUE** *(pushing him)* You are awful! *(giggles)*

**GARY** The baby of course. I just wish I knew how he got here! *(moves downstage right)*

**CLIVE** Time will tell old boy, time will tell. I've often been mystified for months by some action of my wife's. Then in the course of time things are made clear. Sometimes it's best not to ask for explanations.

**BABS** *(enters from the spare bedroom, closing the door)* He's gurgling with contentment after that feed. He was only hungry and in need of a change. *(sits again at desk chair)*

**CLIVE** Aren't we all!

**BABS** He IS a good little thing. Your wife said he was a good baby.

**GARY** But how the hell did she know?

**SUE** Well, she must know whose it is.

**CLIVE** I would say its feminine intuition old boy. They've all got it coming out of their ears.

**GARY** Maybe I should ring Hazel. I'd like to get to the bottom of this baby business!

**SUE** You just 'ave!

**GARY** No, I mean she really shouldn't have done this without telling me. It's not like her.

**CLIVE** Do you mean the baby's not like her?

**GARY** No. I mean it's not like Hazel to make arrangements like this without telling me.

**BABS** Do you know where she's rehearsing?

**GARY** Well, it's usually the Baptist Church Hall.

**BABS** They have bingo there on Fridays. *(yawns)*

**CLIVE** Not for me that bingo lark. Tried it once - was bored out of my skull - the only time I got excited was when they said legs eleven. *(laughs)* Decidedly third class!

**GARY** Hazel said it was an extra rehearsal, so they're probably meeting somewhere else.

**BABS** Must be.

**CLIVE** Anyway, even if you did phone her, what would she do? Come home and interrupt us just when we're all getting acquainted!

*Clive has been trying to edge his arm round Sue and at this point he gives her a squeeze.*

**GARY** I suppose you're right. And she wouldn't thank me for interrupting her rehearsal.

**SUE** An' if she came 'ome, I expect we'd have to scarper! I come 'ere to enjoy meself.

**CLIVE** So did I!

**GARY** Well, what should we do?

**CLIVE** I can think of something!

**GARY** With that baby liable to cry at any moment?

**BABS** I expect he'll drop off to sleep again presently. *(yawns)* I could do the same myself.

**CLIVE** And then we can all take up where we left off!

**BABS** Well I don't know about that, Clive. I'm tired and I've got a headache. I'm good for nothing at the moment.

**SUE** I am! What do you reckon Gary?

**GARY** *(sitting TV chair)* Oh I dunno.

**SUE** There's enthusiasm for you! You don' t have to sound so keen!

**GARY** You must know how I feel Sue, being here in my own house, with Clive and Babs here as well, not to mention a baby!

**CLIVE** *(taking the plunge)* Well I say it's a pity to waste a golden opportunity. Never look a gift horse in the mouth! Seize the moment! *(looks at. Sue)*

**SUE** What you got in mind then?

**CLIVE** *(slowly and looking from one to the other)* Well, if Babs is tired and has a headache... and Gary's got cold feet...

**SUE** I wouldn't know about that! Aint got near enough to find out! 'Ere what are you suggestin'?

**CLIVE** That if you're in the mood, and I'm in the mood...

**SUE** Oh, you are a one! What would Gary say! Gary?

**GARY** I don' t know, I mean, if you, you know... well... I don't know what to say.

**SUE** You don't care much about me do you?

**GARY** I do but it's awkward for me isn't it? I mean I don't want to be inhospitable!

**SUE** What's bein' in 'ospital go to do with it?

*Babs yawns.*

**GARY** Nothing.

**CLIVE** I don't think Babs would mind if Sue and I... er... used up a bit of energy, would you Babs?

**BABS** *(looking daggers)* Oh please yourself... you usually do.

**CLIVE** Excellent, first class. Come on then Sue. *(stands)*

**SUE** Well, I don't know, I mean... I just met you... you aint even bought me a drink!

**CLIVE** I'll give you one, I will, I promise!

**SUE** *(giggling)* Well... What can I say!... All right, you're on mate!

**CLIVE** That's what I call sporting! First class!

**SUE** Come on then sailor boy... where are we going, your place? *(stands and goes to pick up her bag from the table)*

**CLIVE** Good lord no! What's wrong with staying here?

**SUE** Ooh, you are a cheeky devil! Don't waste any time do you? That all right with you Gary? What d'you reckon?

**GARY** *(distastefully)* Oh, be my guests!

**SUE** Oh well, why not? Come on then Popeye! I hope you've been eatin' your spinach!

*She exits to the master bedroom followed by Clive. A few giggles from Sue until they shut the door. Gary and Babs remain seated, thinking. A moment.*

**BABS** Well, there's a turn up! I knew Clive was always ready sort of, but I didn't think he'd be that bold! Good riddance!

**GARY** It's at a time like this that you realise who your friends are!

**BABS** Have you known that Sue long?

**GARY** Oh, I suppose about a year. She turned up at the Queen's Arms to work behind the bar. *(moves to put bed together again)*

**BABS** And how long have you been meeting her?

**GARY** No time at all! Said she'd fancied me for months and tonight she was going to have her wicked way with me! Bit of a narrow escape.

**BABS** If you ask me Gary, and I don't mean to interfere, you're well off without her. Barmaids like her have always got a bit of a reputation as far as men are concerned.

**GARY** You're probably right. I don't know many people here. I only manage to get to the pub on a Friday. I'm often away from home on business. How about you? How long have you and Clive been meeting up?

**BABS** Few months. We met in February at my niece's engagement party. Started chatting me up over the vol-au-vents. And he's quite a chatter-up I can tell you. We arranged to meet but it wasn't easy. Then he suggested I did some babysitting. I expect it was a dodge he's used before. Anyway, I made some arrangements and we've met up at different places. It's been sort of fun really, but I expect he's grown tired of me.

**GARY** And how do you know Hazel?

**BABS** Oh I only met her this evening. My friend Madge works with her. She gave Hazel my number. *(yawns again)*

**GARY** Look here Babs. You're tired. Why don't you get off home?

**BABS** Do you think you could manage the baby by yourself?

**GARY** I could learn!

**BABS** I think I should be here when Hazel comes back.

**GARY** Maybe you're right. Tell you what, go and have a lie down on the spare bed in there. Perhaps forty winks would clear your head. Go on. I'll put this place in order.

**BABS** Sounds like a good idea. I don't specially want to see Clive's face when he comes out of there. *(points to the master bedroom)*

**GARY** Off you go then!

*Babs gets up and wearily goes into spare room, closing the door. Gary has put the sofabed up again and now begins to clear cups and glasses into the kitchen via the hatch. Then the master bedroom door opens.*

**CLIVE** *(entering in boxer shorts)* Excuse me!

**GARY** Everything all right?

**CLIVE** First Class! Just need a leak that's all. When you get to my age when you've got to go, you've got to go!

**GARY** *(moving downstage to put his rugby ball into the basket)* You know where it is... Christ, that sounds like our gate! *(he is beside the 'window' and pulls aside the curtain a little)* That's Hazel - I recognize her jacket! She's with someone!

**CLIVE** What do you think we should do!

**GARY** SShh! Keep your voice down! Why is she back so early! She said she would be late tonight!

**CLIVE** Perhaps she's forgotten something and just come back for it. Is there a way out round the back?

**GARY** There is, but at the moment it's blocked up with rubble! We'll just have to brave it out!

**CLIVE** *(his bravado has deserted him)* You do it! God, I've got an urgent call! I'll hide in the lav! I just hope they go away!

**GARY** What about your clothes?

**CLIVE** Can't worry about them now! First things first! *(exits)*

**GARY** Well you'd better lock yourself in!

*As these lines are said, Hazel and Dan walk silently and slowly up path. Hazel opens her handbag but can't find her door key. Dan maybe produces a pencil torch to help her. In the end she finds it in the pocket of her anorak. They can exchange a few words. Dan is about 40, the strong silent type, tall and fit, a rugged-looking bachelor, dressed in a T shirt, leather jacket, jeans and black boots.*

**HAZEL** Thank God for that. Thought I'd lost it.

**DAN** You know what you've been doing Hazel?

**HAZEL** What's that?

**DAN** Leading me up the garden path.

**HAZEL** *(laughs)* I like your sense of humour! You don't often make wise cracks do you? Rather a dark horse you are.

**DAN** One that you're leading to water?

**HAZEL** That's enough of your punning! Come on. *(reaches for the keyhole)*

**DAN** Er, Hazel.

**HAZEL** *(turns)* What is it?

**DAN** Wait a moment. Are you sure you should invite a strange man into your house? I mean, I know you said that your husband was out, but what would the neighbours think?

*Dan leans casually against the wheely bin and they converse on the doorstep, a conversation which Gary tries unsuccessfully to hear.*

**HAZEL** We hardly know the neighbours... and even if we did, what is there to worry about? It's all perfectly innocent! We need somewhere to rehearse and that pub was much too noisy. Anyway, I forgot my script so we came back here! What's wrong with that?

**DAN** Well, it sounds plausible enough I suppose.

**HAZEL** It's the truth isn't it? I told Gary I had a rehearsal, so, even if he comes back early - which is highly unlikely - it'll be OK. There's no problem.

**DAN** Did you tell him that I was the only member of the group you were meeting?

**HAZEL** Well no, not exactly. *(sits on the bench)* I just said it was an extra rehearsal. He's not much interested in my drama work.

**DAN** And do you trust me? I might be a serial killer! Do you want to be alone in the house with me?

**HAZEL** I think I know you well enough Dan. Besides, we won't be alone. There's a friend of mine here so we'll have to send her home first. She might get in the way.

**DAN** Get in what way?

**HAZEL** Er... of the rehearsal of course! What else? *(stands)* Come on, I've also got a surprise for you.

**DAN** Really? What sort of surprise?

**HAZEL** I can't show you on the doorstep!

**DAN** Well, all right, I'm a sucker for surprises.

*Hazel reaches up to open the door as Gary scuttles into the kitchen. Dan follows her in and closes the door. Hazel looks around for Babs.*

**HAZEL** Funny! She's not here. Think I know where she'll be.

*Hazel goes into the spare room while Dan takes a look at the bookcase. She re-enters without her jacket and quietly closes the door.*

**HAZEL** She's fallen asleep on the spare bed. She said she was tired. She must have been cold too, she's wearing my dressing gown. We'll let her sleep it off.

**DAN** Won't we be disturbing her?

**HAZEL** Not if we keep our voices down. *(comes to join him)* She's out like a light. *(sniffs)* Can you smell smoke?

**DAN** You've been eating chips!

**HAZEL** Didn't know Babs was a smoker.

**DAN** I see you're a great rugby enthusiast!

**HAZEL** Oh yes, you just don't know what the sight of all those thick male thighs does to me! When I see them all straining in the scrum I go weak at the knees!

**DAN** Seriously?

**HAZEL** No, you idiot. That's Gary's hobby. Not playing you realise, not now. He can sit for hours and watch re-plays of all the matches he's recorded. Not just the internationals either.

**DAN** Used to play a bit myself.

**HAZEL** You've certainly got the build. You should take it up again.

**DAN** I might go down to the local club some Saturday. Just to watch mind you. I think my playing days are over.

**HAZEL** *(pause)* Now, how about a drink?

**DAN** Oh no thanks, I'm all right.

**HAZEL** Go on, you only had a half pint in the pub. That's not enough for a strapping big chap like you!

**DAN** Oh all right. I'll have a coffee please.

*Hazel says "Right" and sets off for the kitchen but at the door turns back.*

**HAZEL** What am I doing? Let's have something alcoholic. I'm tired of tea and coffee. Drink it all day at work. What do you say?

**DAN** I'll have what you have then.

**HAZEL** Now you're talking! You sit and make yourself comfortable.

*Hazel makes for the drinks table and Dan wanders across to look at the photos above the desk.*

**DAN** I like your house Hazel.

**HAZEL** It's not much but, as they say, we call it home.

**DAN** It's very pleasant I think. Quiet, and orderly. *(studying a photo)* You're quite a star in the-group aren't you?

**HAZEL** I wouldn't say that. I've been lucky to get some good parts in the last few productions that's all.

**DAN** I think you're being modest. I joined just before the last production and you were very good. And I didn't only have the evidence of my eyes - people talk you know. *(sits at desk)*

**HAZEL** Oh I do. When I joined the group about four years ago I think I heard everyone's life story within weeks. All the parts they'd had, in all the different plays stretching back I don't know how long. *(brings the drinks to the sofabed)* Come and sit over here Dan. It's more comfortable! *(sits TV end)*

**DAN** Am I not all right where I am?

**HAZEL** We can't rehearse at opposite ends of the room can we? And we don't want to wake Babs up. Come on, we're supposed to be husband and wife!

**DAN** You win again. *(gets up and crosses to the sofabed)*

**HAZEL** *(handing him his drink)* That's for you. Cheers!

**DAN** Your good health Hazel!

**HAZEL** Here's to a dramatic relationship!

**DAN** Well, that's one way of putting it.

*Hazel clinks her glass with his and they drink.*

**DAN** What's this you've given me?

**HAZEL** Only a mild drug mixed in with some ginger ale.

**DAN** Oh that's all right then. For a moment I thought you were trying to make me incapable.

**HAZEL** Now why would I want to do that? *(laughs)*

*Hazel gets up and goes over to the Hi Fi. She presses on the tape she had primed before she went out. She then comes quickly back to sit beside Dan.*

**DAN** Aren't we going to read our scripts then?

**HAZEL** There's no hurry. See if you like my new tape. I think it's great. I first heard this when I was ...

*She is interrupted by the loud haka that Gary has played. She jumps to her feet and switches it off.*

**DAN** Are you trying to wake your friend up?

**HAZEL** No, I don't understand this.

**DAN** Don't tell me you want to do a tribal dance.

**HAZEL** Oh no ... never mind. *(returns to the sofabed somewhat puzzled)* I was playing a tape before I went out.

**DAN** Is everything all right?

**HAZEL** Er yes, it's... oh, Babs must have played some music - though that wouldn't have put her to sleep!... So, Dan, *(smiles)* in your short time with the group, you've learnt all about everyone?

**DAN** Not really. People are friendly but I've not asked lots of questions. *(realising)* Oh, I'm sorry Hazel. I didn't mean that you'd been nosy.

**HAZEL** Don't worry. I know you weren't criticising me. I suppose I am curious about people when I first meet them. You for instance.

**DAN** Me?

**HAZEL** Well, you've only been with us since June, and what with the summer break, I don't think I've got to know you as well as I'd like.

**DAN** There's not a lot to know.

**HAZEL** I can't believe that! For example, what brought you to this part of the world?

**DAN** That's easy. My firm was opening a new branch office and asked for volunteers to be transferred to it. I thought about it for a while and put my name forward. I've no ties you see, so it was easier for me than for some of the married guys.

**HAZEL** How very noble of you.

**DAN** Well they made it worth my while.

**HAZEL** What does this firm of yours do?

**DAN** Architects. I spend most of my time in the drawing office hunched over plans. That's partly why I like to get out in the evenings.

**HAZEL** I see... So, it's true then.

**DAN** What's true?

**HAZEL** Well, I'd heard that you weren't married.

**DAN** That's no secret. I must have told some people.

**HAZEL** You do have secrets then? Tell me some!

**DAN** Don't you think we should rehearse? *(gets out script from his jacket pocket)*

**HAZEL** Must we? Just tell me a bit more first! How Is it that a very eligible bachelor like you hasn't been snapped up by some predatory female?

**DAN** What makes you think I'm eligible?

**HAZEL** Well you're quite a looker, as they say. You've a good steady job, newish car, you dress stylishly... need I go on?

**DAN** Just what predatory females are looking for eh? Appearances aren't everything.

**HAZEL** I bet you've got a string of girlfriends already in this area, hidden away in lonely bedsits, waiting for the evening of the week when it's their turn for you to call!

**DAN** You've quite an imagination! Suppose I tell you that I've been married four times?

**HAZEL** I wouldn't believe you!

**DAN** *(laughs)* You'd be quite right... No, I've not been, as you say, snapped up!

**HAZEL** *(flirtatiously)* What big teeth I have! *(bears them at him)*

**DAN** Look here, Red Riding Hood, what would your husband have to say if he found us here, with you grinning at a wolf? Wouldn't he reach for the nearest axe?

**HAZEL** Do you know, I've never really thought about that. Gary's a very easy-going sort of chap. A bit too easy-going. I don't know if jealousy is part of his make-up. I've never put him to the test.

**DAN** I think we should get on with rehearsing.

**HAZEL** But this is such a cosy chat. Much more interesting than the play. This new one's a bit of a bore. Talking to you is far more entertaining. I like getting to know you better.

**DAN** As you get to know me better, you may like me less. And I'm sure you haven't forgotten that you're a married woman.

**HAZEL** Don't remind me, I know. *(gets up)*

**DAN** I'm sorry if it's not a happy marriage.

**HAZEL** *(going downstage left)* Oh, I suppose it's as happy as most marriages these days. We jog along. I think we need children, or at least I do. Maybe that's the problem, or my problem. Life has been much the same for some time. I need something to give me a a bit of excitement.

**DAN** Doesn't Gary want children then?

**HAZEL** I think his excuse is we can't afford them. But being a dad would do him good. I'm sure he'd enjoy it. And make him be a bit more responsible. *(returns to the sofabed)* Would you like to have children?

**DAN** Oh, I don't think I'm cut out for it.

**HAZEL** The gossip isn't true is it?

**DAN** What gossip is that?

**HAZEL** That you're not really interested in women.

*He gets up to move downstage left.*

That's what some people are saying.

**DAN** Hazel, just because a guy isn't married doesn't mean he isn't interested in women. I am, but since you seem keen to know everything about me, you might as well know that in certain respects I prefer the company of men. *(slight pause)* We don't all have limp wrists you know.

**HAZEL** I see ... I'm sorry.

**DAN** Don't be sorry for my sake. I'm very happy as I am.

**HAZEL** I'm pleased to hear it, and I still think you're great!

**DAN** Now, do you think we'd better rehearse?

**HAZEL** OK Dan. I'll get my script.

*Hazel goes to the bookcase and collects her script. as Dan sits again. She returns and they flick through pages.*

**HAZEL** Here we are, page nine, that's the first bit we do alone together. You go from "I can't go on ... "

**DAN** How can I go, if I can't go on?

**HAZEL** Very funny! Right!

*During this reading, which despite the corny script they take very seriously, they raise their voices to project. Gary quietly opens hatch to watch, listen and react. They hold their scripts low so that Gary doesn't see they're reading.*

**DAN** "I can't go on meeting you like this darling."

**HAZEL** "But why? Isn't this best under the circumstances?"

**DAN** "I've made my mind up. I know what I'm going to do."

**HAZEL** "What?"

**DAN** "I'm going to give myself up!"

**HAZEL** "But why? They'll put you away for years! I know you only acted in self-defence, but will a jury believe you?"

**DAN** "That's a chance I'll have to take. What I've told you is true. I didn't mean to kill him! If only he hadn't got in the way!

*They quietly turn a page of script, and Gary moves from the hatch to open the door, the rolling pin again in his hand.*

**HAZEL** "Then you're determined to go to the police?"

**DAN** "Yes, I know that if I'm found guilty I may be separated from you for years but that's better than to keep meeting you for a few stolen moments while I'm on the run."

**HAZEL** "Oh darling, darling! When shall I see you again?"

**DAN** "Why did this have to happen to us?" *(puts his arm round her)*

**HAZEL** "Hold me close! Swear that you love me!"

**DAN** "You know I do!"

**HAZEL** "Then tell me!"

**DAN** "I love you!"

**HAZEL** "Darling!"

*Hazel throws her arms round the startled Dan and kisses him. Gary reacts with horror but he is clearly at a loss about what to do. He can't stand the sight of Hazel with Dan, but thinks Dan is a gangster. Dan then firmly but gently pushes Hazel back until she is at arms' length.*

**HAZEL** "Before you go my darling, my surprise. Would you like to see the baby?"

*That's enough for Gary. He bangs the table, raises the rolling pin and advances with as much threat as he dare.*

**GARY** *(behind sofabed)* That's enough! I've heard enough!
**HAZEL** Gary! What are you doing here?

*Hazel and Dan have put their scripts down and Hazel has jumped to her feet and backed towards the TV unit.*

**GARY** Well may you ask! I've caught you redhanded. Been having an affair with a... with a... criminal Have you"?
**HAZEL** He's not a criminal!
**GARY** Oh no?
**HAZEL** Dan, this is my husband, Gary.
**DAN** *(rising and towering over Gary)* How do you do? *(offers a handshake)*
**GARY** *(ignoring the hand)* I'll tell you how I do! *(turns on Hazel)* You you ... hussy! Now I know who the baby in there belongs to!
**HAZEL** No, I don't think you do.
**GARY** Don't try to deny it!
**HAZEL** You don't think it's mine do you?
**GARY** You've ... you've adopted it ... that's right ... you've adopted it behind my back!
**HAZEL** *(moving downstage right)* And how could I possibly have adopted it?
**GARY** I knew you were keen to have kids but this is going too far!
**HAZEL** I tell you it's not my baby!
**GARY** Whose is it then? *(throwing a glare at Dan)* His?
**DAN** Just leave me out of this!
**GARY** Typical! *(moves towards Dan)* Trying to avoid your responsibilities!
**HAZEL** I brought it here, from work.
**GARY** Oh! Bringing our work home now are we? *(moving back to Hazel)*
**HAZEL** One of the mothers pleaded with me to look after it for her.
**GARY** Why didn't she ask someone else?
**HAZEL** She couldn't find someone else!
**GARY** Oh yes, and why may I ask?
**HAZEL** Her husband's in prison and she needed to visit him.
**GARY** Oh really? Overnight?
**HAZEL** Yes! The prison's too far for her to reach in a day. The authorities never seem to consider where a family lives when they lock somebody up.
**GARY** Her husband is one of your mates is he? *(moves towards Dan)*
**DAN** I asked you to leave me out of this!

**GARY** Prison indeed! Do you honestly expect me to believe that?

**HAZEL** It's true I tell you!

**GARY** I've heard enough! You ... you ... deserve a good ... *(raises the rolling pin and begins to move towards Hazel with it)*

**DAN** Hold it there Gary! *(takes the rolling pin from behind)*

**GARY** You wanted to be kept out of this, mate!

**DAN** *(with authority)* Yes, well now I want in! I told you to stop! I've killed a man twice your size!

*Dan, staying in role for the occasion, not only overwhelms Gary by his size and words, but he also puzzles Hazel.*

**GARY** Go on then, do your worst.

**HAZEL** Dan, are you serious?

**DAN** Trust me, I know what I'm doing.

**GARY** *(returning to attack Hazel verbally)* Before this gangster friend of yours puts me out of my misery, just tell me something Hazel. If your story IS true and you just brought the baby here overnight, why on earth didn't you tell me?

**HAZEL** I didn't think that you would co-operate.

**GARY** What makes you say that?

**HAZEL** I thought you'd try to insist I stayed in to look after it.

**GARY** And why couldn't you?

**HAZEL** I wanted to go out.

**GARY** Oh yes.

**HAZEL** I wanted to rehearse.

**GARY** Rehearse? Is that what you call it? You just wanted to carry on with ... with ... desperate Dan here!

**DAN** Watch it you! We DID need to rehearse.

**GARY** Oh yeah? A likely story.

**DAN** It's the truth. I play Hazel's husband.

**GARY** I bet you do! Listen, mate, she's got a husband already.

**DAN** Of course she has, that's you.

**GARY** I know it's bloody me! She doesn't need another one!

**HAZEL** It's only a play Gary.

**GARY** Sure. What is it then?

**DAN** It's called "On the Run."

**GARY** Oh I bet! A play where you don't need any scripts because you know all the lines already! And the actions!

**HAZEL** But there ARE scripts!

**GARY** Where are they then?

**DAN** There!

*Dan points to the scripts at each side of the sofabed. Gary looks, sees them and some of the steam is taken out of him.*

**GARY** You mean that what I heard was you ... reading?

HAZEL Of course we were.

GARY  Then ... then ... *(to Dan)* you're not a murderer?

DAN Only when I'm provoked. *(taps the rolling pin in his palm)*

*Gary and Dan glare at each other until Gary looks away and turns to Hazel.*

GARY  Well, it's the first time you've ever rehearsed here.

HAZEL I know it is.

GARY You might've said you were coming back.

HAZEL I didn't think that ... but it was very noisy where we were.

GARY And why didn't the others come here?

HAZEL Well, the group often splits into smaller units to rehearse.

GARY Especially groups of two eh? *(looks at Dan who is drifting upstage centre)*

HAZEL That depends on the script of course.

GARY  I'm sure it does.

HAZEL You should know that, but you never take any interest.

GARY  You should still have said you might be coming here.

HAZEL Oh, I didn't think you'd mind. I'm sorry, Gary.

GARY  Yeah, well, all right then.

HAZEL Besides, you're usually at the pub on Fridays ... yes, come to think of it, why aren't you there now?

GARY *(turning and moving away downstage left)* Oh ... er ... yes, well I went there as you know, but then I developed this awful headache and ... *(holds his brow)*

HAZEL *(going to him with sympathy)* Oh I'm sorry darling. *(holds him)* No wonder you got overexcited. There now, it's all right.

GARY It's nothing really.

HAZEL I've got some paracetamol in the bedroom. You just sit down quietly and I'll go and fetch them.

GARY *(holding tighter)* No, I'll be all right Hazel. I just need a ... good cuddle!

HAZEL Let me go you idiot! *(breaks free laughing)* We've got a visitor! Why don't you and Dan get acquainted while I go and fetch the pills.

*Gary exchanges a look of anxiety with Dan who comes to shake hands again as Hazel goes into the master bedroom.*

DAN How do you do then Gary?

GARY Yes, fine, er sorry about the mix up.

*They shake hands. Hazel is in the bedroom just long enough to turn round and come out again. She advances on Gary and screams at him*

HAZEL What's that woman doing crouching behind the door?

GARY Er ... What's she doing? *(backing away downstage left)*

HAZEL Yes.

GARY Well you said she was crouching behind the door!

**HAZEL** Very funny! Who is she?

**GARY** Well I don't know that much about her really.

**HAZEL** Oh you don't do you?

**GARY** No, not a lot.

**HAZEL** Why is she half-naked?

**GARY** Perhaps the central heating's on too high?

**HAZEL** Gary?!?

**GARY** Her dress got wet and she took it off to dry it?

**HAZEL** Gary?!?!?!

**GARY** She's a secret exhibitionist?

**HAZEL** Maybe I'll get some sense out of HER!

*Hazel storms into the master bedroom. A scream from Sue who has been grabbed by the hair. Hazel drags her on her hands and knees into the living room on to the rug.*

**HAZEL** Who is this woman?

**GARY** I ... er ...

**SUE** Don't you "this woman" me!

**HAZEL** Come on Gary. I think you owe me an explanation!

**GARY** Well, I ... you see it was like this ... that is

**SUE** You've pulled out some of me 'air you 'ave!

**HAZEL** Oh, shut up, you ... you ... tart!

**SUE** Oo are you callin' a tart?

**HAZEL** I'm Gary's wife if you must know!

**SUE** Poor sod!

**HAZEL** And just what do you mean by that?

**SUE** 'Avin' to put up with the likes of you!

**GARY** *(trying to intervene)* Ladies, pl ...

**HAZEL** Ladies? Ladies? Do you call this thing a lady?

**SUE** Well I don't go round pullin' people's 'air out by the roots!

**HAZEL** I'll pull more than your hair if you're not careful!

**SUE** Get away from me! You're mad! *(scrambles to Gary)* Gary, protect me from 'er! She's bonkers!

*Hazel tries to attack Sue who is somewhat shielded by Gary who tries to hold Hazel away. All three ad lib noisily.*

**DAN** *(stepping up from downstage centre)* Pipe down all of you! Let's have a bit of calm! If there's to be any more violence - and I sincerely hope there isn't - then I'll do it!

**SUE** Blimey! 'Oos 'e? A copper?

**GARY** No he isn't ... or at least I don't think he is. This is Dan.

**SUE** What's 'e want then?

**DAN** I want some peace and quiet.

**GARY** Never you mind Sue ... *(to Hazel who is pacing angrily downstage right)* Hazel, will you relax?

**HAZEL** Relax you say? You want me to relax when behind my back I find you've brought HER into our home?

**SUE** I gotta name you know! I'm not an 'ER. I'm Sue!

**HAZEL** Well, I'm going to do more than sue by the time I've finished!

**SUE** Oh yeah? You an' whose army? *(standing up)*

**HAZEL** Have you two been misbehaving? *(pause)* You and my husband?

**GARY** Well, no actually, I think that ...

**HAZEL** What have you been up to? If you think that I ...

**SUE** What if we 'ave been misbe'aving? Wotcha gonna do about it?

**HAZEL** Dan? We need more violence! Hit them!

*Dan, who had drifted upstage again, advances on Gary who retreats towards the kitchen for some means of escape or protection.*

**GARY** Now Dan, old man, take it easy now!

**SUE** I'm gettin' out of this! *(crosses straight to bathroom)*

**DAN** Oh I don't think I'll hurt you very much.

**GARY** Well, just keep your distance then!

**SUE** *(trying the bathroom door)* It's locked! 'Oo's in there?

**HAZEL** *(from downstage right)* Don't tell me he's got another woman locked in the bathroom!

**SUE** *(banging on door)* Let me in will ya!

*Hazel, by the TV, and Gary and Dan, by the kitchen, turn to see the bathroom door open, and Clive, naked except for boxer shorts, steps in.*

**CLIVE** *(with great assurance)* Sue! There you are! Darling! *(grabs her in an embrace and kisses her)*

**HAZEL** What the blazes!

**DAN** This house is unbelievable!

**HAZEL** What IS going on in my home!

*The brief clinch of Clive and Sue having ended, Sue turns to see Hazel still threatening her. She immediately returns Clive's embrace.*

**SUE** Clive! Keep 'er away from me!

**HAZEL** Clive? Who's Clive?

**GARY** He's Clive.

**CLIVE** I'm Clive.

**SUE** This is Clive.

**CLIVE** *(to Sue)* I wondered where you'd gone my pretty.

**SUE** Well, I'm 'ere now! *(another hug)*

**HAZEL** Gary, I'm talking to you! What are these people doing here?

**DAN** Come on Gary, it's time you explained a few things! *(patting the rolling pin in his palm)* Hazel deserves an answer.

**GARY** *(moving downstage)* Well, it's er ... quite simple really ... They had obviously lost each other ... and ... are now together again!

**HAZEL** Brilliant! How did they get in here?

**GARY** They were ... looking for each other?

**HAZEL** Oh. Gary, for goodness' sake, talk sense!

**CLIVE** *(coming forward)* Perhaps I should explain. You must be Hazel. *(offers hand and Hazel puts her hands on her hips)* Allow me to introduce myself. I'm ... er ... Clive. And this is Sue.

**HAZEL** She and I have already met!

**SUE** Yeah, worst luck!

**CLIVE** Yes, well you see it was like this. Gary here had nothing to do with it. You can take my word for it.

**HAZEL** You mean you two came together?

**SUE** *(to Clive)* Chance would be a fine thing!

**HAZEL** I mean you came here together!

**CLIVE** 'Course we did!

**HAZEL** *(goes to Gary and sees that Dan is standing by)* Gary.

**DAN** Do you still want me to hit him?

**HAZEL** No, wait Dan. *(taking Gary downstage left)* I'm sorry Gary. The whole thing is so confusing. I didn't mean to doubt you. Can you forgive me?

**GARY** Oh, yes, I think so.

**HAZEL** You're not sure?

**GARY** Well it's all a bit sudden like. I've just forgiven you once.

**HAZEL** And you with that terrible headache.

**CLIVE** He's got a bad headache too?

**HAZEL** Who else has got one?

**CLIVE** Oh, er... I mean it's too bad he's got a headache.

**HAZEL** He went down the pub to play darts ... *(turns from Clive to Gary)* Did you let the team down Gary?

**GARY** Oh, they didn't need me after all! Then I developed this bit of a head so, I er, thought I'd come home, have an early night.

**HAZEL** All by yourself, and on a Friday too?

**GARY** Well, er... I suppose you could say that.

**HAZEL** And I wasn't here to look after you. Poor Gary.

**SUE** Yeah, poor Gary!

**HAZEL** I'm sorry Sue. You can understand how I felt finding you here.

**SUE** Oh, that's all right, 'azel. Don't mention it.

**HAZEL** These mistakes do happen.

**SUE** Yeah, they do 'appen.

**DAN** *(picking up script on his way to the door)* Well, I'm glad you seem to have sorted matters out, so, if you don't mind, I think I'll be on my way.

**HAZEL** *(turning to him)* Oh you needn't go just yet Dan.

**DAN** We can rehearse our lines some other time.

**SUE** (coming downstage right) Cor, is 'e in your drama club?

**DAN** Yes I am.

**SUE** I wouldn't mind bein' in the club! *(giggles)* Whatever am I sayin?

**HAZEL** *(to Dan)* Have a drink before you go. Help yourself.

**CLIVE** Yes, do!

**SUE** Yeah, do!

*Dan moves to drinks table.*

**GARY** *(sitting on beanbag)* No, don't!

**HAZEL** Don't be inhospitable Gary.

**SUE** Look, who's been in 'ospital then?

**HAZEL** It's nothin Sue.

**SUE** You ain't pregnant again, are ya? *(giggles)*

**HAZEL** *(laughs)* Oh no, we've sorted all that out haven't we Gary?

**GARY** *(laughing too)* Oh yes, no problems there now.

**CLIVE** *(laughingly)* Yes, under the circumstances, the best thing really is to have a good laugh and all be friends! *(his arm is round Sue)*

*The tension has eased again somewhat. Gary laughs a bit nervously. He knows Babs is still to appear.*

**HAZEL** You know, there's still something I don't understand. *(to Gary)* How did Clive and Sue get in here?

**CLIVE** *(thinking on his feet again. Steps toward)* Well, it was like this ... you see ...

**SUE** *(stepping up behind him)* We was out for a walk!

**CLIVE** *(steps again)* Yes, it was a lovely late summer's evening and we thought that a walk would be pleasant so ...

**SUE** *(steps again)* We come down your street!

**CLIVE** Yes ... we don't often walk in this direction, but tonight we decided to see what these houses were like and ...

**SUE** We liked this 'ouse!

**CLIVE** *(centre stage)* Sue?

**SUE** I said we liked the look of this 'ouse didn't we Clive!

**CLIVE** Yes, you did, that was what you said, yes indeed ... First class house you said, so ...

**SUE** So we thought we'd 'ave a closer look!

**CLIVE** Er yes, we wondered whether ...

**HAZEL** Do you know, I've heard enough of this nonsense. I'm going to wake up Babs. I left her in charge here. I think she's got some explaining to do! *(breaks from Gary and goes into the spare room)*

**GARY** *(to Clive)* Nice bit of invention that Clive!

**SUE** Clever ain't we? I 'elped! *(hugs Clive)*

**GARY** Well, don't overdo it! Hazel has gone to fetch Babs! What do we do now?

**DAN** *(moving to sit at desk chair)* Who on earth is Babs?

**SUE** She came 'ere to babysit, more like babysleep!

**GARY** What do we do now Clive? If Babs blabs and says that she came here with you, how are you going to explain what you've just said about coming here with Sue?

**SUE** If Babs blabs! I like it!

**GARY** Well Clive?

**CLIVE** We'll think of something. Play it by ear. I don't think Hazel is the sort to be angry for long.

**GARY** Psychologist as well are you? Well we won't have long to wait. Here they come!

**SUE** Quite excitin' really aint it?

*Clive and Sue separate as Hazel enters helping the sleepy Babs.*

**HAZEL** Now Babs, perhaps you could sort something out for me.

**BABS** Don't rush me Hazel. I don't know when I've had a deeper sleep.

**HAZEL** Take your time then, there's no hurry.

**BABS** Thank goodness tomorrow's Saturday. I can sleep in.

*Hazel leads Babs towards the sofabed. Babs does not see Dan.*

**BABS** If you don't mind, I'll have a hard chair. Don't want to doze off again. *(heads for the chair to right of the table)*

*Hazel turns it to face towards Clive and Sue.*

What is it then dear?

**HAZEL** Well, in the first place, do you know these people?

**BABS** Oh ... yes ... that you Clive?

**CLIVE** I should say so old girl.

**HAZEL** You know him?

**BABS** Oh yes, only too well. Why have you let me sleep so long?

**CLIVE** I ... had other matters on my hands!

**BABS** Oh yes, *(looking at Sue)* I remember now. *(with a touch of malice)* Has he been looking after you dear?

**SUE** 'E aint had much chance! *(sits TV chair)*

**HAZEL** What I'd like to know Babs is how they got in here.

**GARY** *(getting desperate)* Hazel, what does it matter? Babs is tired I don't think that... um... we need to go into all that now.

**HAZEL** Oh don't you, indeed? *(advancing to Gary)*

**GARY** No I don't. What's done is best ...

**HAZEL** Is best explained! YOU may understand what's going in our home Gary but I don't! *(turning)* Well Babs? How did this Clive get here?

**BABS** *(not unhappy that she's probably "shopping" Clive)* Well ... when you left me here, I'm sorry, but I let him in.

**HAZEL** And did he bring Sue?

**CLIVE** I'm sure she remembers that I did, eh Babs?

**HAZEL** Well? What do you remember?

**BABS** Er, my head's not at all clear, you see ... I had this drink and ...

**CLIVE** Then there was a knock at the door and Sue and I were there! Isn't that right Babs?

**BABS** Clive, I don't think that we should ...

**HAZEL** Keep out Clive, she's doing all right.

**SUE** *(standing)* Well everyone, I think I ought to be toddling off!

**HAZEL** *(firmly)* You'll toddle off when I tell you to toddle off!

**SUE** *(stung)* Ooo pardon me, I'm sure! *(sits again)*

*Slowly, Hazel turns towards Gary on beanbag. He cowers noticeably.*

**HAZEL** Gary?

**GARY** Yes dear?

**HAZEL** Did you by any chance bring Sue here?

**GARY** What? Did I bring Sue here'? Is that what you're asking?

**HAZEL** *(icily)* That is precisely what I'm asking.

**GARY** And you want the truth?

**HAZEL** Yes Gary, if it's not too much to ask.

**GARY** Well ... I ... No, I didn't actually!

**HAZEL** And that's the truth?

**GARY** Yes! As true as true can be.

**HAZEL** *(puts her hands on Gary's shoulders)* Well that's a relief! *(pause)* But if YOU didn't, who did?

*A moment's pause.*

**SUE** *(retaliating)* Gary's right ya know. 'E didn't bring me 'ere.

**HAZEL** No?

**SUE** No, 'e didn't... it was me what brung 'IM 'ere!

**HAZEL** *(moving towards Sue)* Oh, you did, did you?

**SUE** 'Sright!

**HAZEL** *(moving to Clive)* And so Babs let you in alone?

**CLIVE** Well, if you put it like th...

**HAZEL** And why may I ask? *(moving to Babs)* And Babs ... What are you wearing under my dressing gown

**BABS** Not a lot dear. I'm sorry Hazel.

**HAZEL** So am I! There's some kind of orgy been going on in my house while I've been out! *(to Sue and Clive)* If different people brought you here, why are you both in your underwear?

**SUE** Well, if you must know, we fancied ... a bit of a lie down.

**CLIVE** We needed a little rest!

**HAZEL** In my home? May you rest, in peace! Dan?

**BABS** *(turning)* Who's Dan?

**SUE** 'E's Dan!

**DAN** I'm Dan.

**HAZEL** He's a good friend of mine.
**DAN** What is it?
**HAZEL** Violence please! *(points at Gary)* Start with him!

*Dan is sitting at the desk at this point and not reacting. Hazel approaches him as Gary scampers towards Sue. Their interaction, and that of the other pair may begin separately but then more rapidly overlap as all ad lib to reach a crescendo when the bell rings.*

**HAZEL** *(incensed, to Dan)* Aren't you going to do something?
**DAN** *(to Hazel)* Well, you don't really want me to hurt him do you?
**BABS** *(standing to argue upstage centre with Clive)* Why did you give me such a strong drink?
**CLIVE** *(to Babs)* I thought it would help you to relax!
**GARY** *(downstage right with Sue)* See what you've done saying that?
**SUE** *(to Gary)* Well it's the truth in it?
**DAN** *(to Hazel)* We came her to rehearse, don't you remember?
**HAZEL** *(to Dan)* This is much more important!
**BABS** *(to Clive)* Practically knocked me out!
**CLIVE** *(to Babs)* I thought you could hold your drink!
**GARY** *(to Sue)* I don't know why I let you persuade me to come here in the first place!
**SUE** *(to Gary)* Well you know what you wanted dontcha?
**BABS** *(to Clive)* Fancy behaving with Sue like that!
**CLIVE** *(to Babs)* You had a headache, remember?
**DAN** *(to Hazel)* Well, if we're not rehearsing, I'd better go.
**HAZEL** *(to Dan)* I don't want us to part in this atmosphere.
**GARY** *(to Sue)* I didn't want you coming here to make a fool of yourself!
**SUE** *(to Gary)* I suppose you can do that on yer own!
**BABS** *(to Clive)* Well you better take me home now Hazel's here.
**CLIVE** *(to Babs)* Typical, just because you don't feel well, I have to go!
**DAN** *(to Hazel)* We'll be meeting again on Tuesday!
**HAZEL** *(coming downstage centre and turning Gary round)* See what a riot you've caused bringing that tart into the house?

*This move of Hazel's is the cue for the bell to ring. The ringer is Sam, a very smartly turned out young police constable who has walked swiftly up the path. At the bell, the arguments dry up.*

**GARY** Who can that be?
**HAZEL** Some other tart from the pub no doubt. *(looks exchanged with Sue)*
**GARY** Or some other Adonis from the drama club.

*Dan glares.*

**HAZEL** For goodness' sake open it!

*He does so. Sam is standing at the foot of the steps. Gary reacts.*

**SAM** Good evening Sir, Sorry to trouble you.
**GARY** Oh, er, good evening officer.
**SAM** I'm PC Cornwall. May I come in a moment Sir?

*Sue giggles.*

**GARY** Oh, er, yes, of course.

*As Sam enters, Clive, who has recognised her voice and glimpsed her uniform, nips into the bathroom. Sam enters with brisk dignity and moves towards the master bedroom door and turns so that she can take in the other five occupants. Hazel sits on sofabed.*

**SAM** Good evening everyone. Sorry to break into a party like this.
**HAZEL** Oh, there's no party.
**SUE** Wish there was!
**HAZEL** Quiet you!
**GARY** Er, how can we help you officer?
**SAM** Is everyone in the house present?
**GARY** Why do you ask?
**SAM** It's just that as I came in, I thought I saw somebody disappearing into that room.
**BABS** *(looking behind her)* Where's Clive?
**SAM** Exactly! Would you mind asking him to come in here madam?
**BABS** *(banging on door)* Clive, you're wanted!
**CLIVE** *(with put on accent)* You'll have to wait. I'm busy for a few minutes!

*General reaction to this.*

**GARY** *(taking off Clive's strange voice)* Do you hear that? You'll have to wait. I'm busy for a few minutes!
**SAM** We can wait that long. *(sniffs and looks around)*
**HAZEL** What is it officer?
**SAM** Have you been ... Oh, nothing ... Would the rest of you please sit down?

*Dan stays in the chair at the desk, Babs is at the table, Sue sits on the chair by the TV, Hazel is on sofabed, and Gary is about to sit beside her when they exchange looks and he moves to the beanbag. A moment.*

**BABS** Come on Clive, we're waiting!
**CLIVE** *(in the voice)* Just hold on can't you?
**BABS** *(to Sam)* He's in the loo you see. He's had a fair amount to drink and you know that when men reach a certain age, they tend to have trouble with their waterworks.

**SAM** So I've been told, thank you madam.

*The toilet flushes and Clive emerges looking rather sheepish.*

**CLIVE** *(nervously)* Oh, er, hello Sam!
**SAM** I thought it was you, Mr Cornwall.
**CLIVE** Mr Cornwall? Mr Cornwall? I'm your dad for God's sake!

*Reaction.*

**SAM** And I'm on duty Sir. So this is one of your hideouts?
**CLIVE** What on earth do you mean?
**SAM** Just out of interest, which one of these ladies is she?
**CLIVE** Which one of these ladies is what?
**SAM** Well, your current mistress of course.
**CLIVE** Oh, er, you know then?
**SAM** *(pleasantly)* We've all known for years, and years.
**CLIVE** My God! Have you really?
**GARY** So much for the covering of tracks, eh Clive? *(laughs)*
**SAM** Well who is the lucky lady?
**BABS** Well, he came here with me officer.
**SAM** *(moving upstage to her)* So you must be Babs. You have my sympathy madam.
**BABS** That's no way to speak about your father!
**SAM** At the moment madam he's just another member of the public. *(to Clive)* I think you ought to get some clothes on, don't you Sir?
**BABS** Yes, come on Clive. Let's make ourselves decent.

*Babs and the crestfallen Clive go into the master bedroom.*

**SAM** *(moving to Sue)* Under the circumstances madam, I'm sure I don't know why you're wearing next to nothing.
**SUE** Mind yer own business!
**SAM** I see.
**HAZEL** Officer, this visit of yours ... there hasn't been a report of a missing baby has there?
**SAM** *(taking out her notebook)* Have you lost a baby then madam?
**GARY** She hasn't exactly had one yet!
**HAZEL** Oh be quiet you.
**SAM** Well madam?
**HAZEL** No, I haven't lost one but it's just that I'm looking after a baby tonight for someone whose husband has a police record.
**SAM** Do you mean her husband is on the run?
**DAN** Well he was, a few minutes ago, in the play!
**SAM** *(moving behind sofabed towards Dan)* So I've interrupted a play reading have I?

**HAZEL** No not really, ignore that remark officer. No, the father of the baby I'm looking after is in prison.

**SAM** *(from behind sofabed)* And the mother?

**HAZEL** She's visiting her husband.

**SAM** That seems a very public spirited act, if I may say so madam.

*Sue suddenly puts her hands over her face, falls on her knees and yells.*

**SUE** I confess!

*All eyes turn.*

I give meself up!

**GARY** And not for the first time, I bet!

**SAM** (turning to Sue) Madam?

**SUE** You've come 'ere for me ain't you?

**SAM** I beg your pardon madam? *(moves downstage towards Sue)*

**SUE** I always meant to pay! I just never got around to it!

**SAM** Would you mind explaining?

**SUE** It's me poll tax in it? I never put me name on the ... the registrar did I, so I thought that I could, you know, get off with it.

**GARY** Or get off with somebody!

**SAM** (to Gary) Please Sir, no more interruptions. *(to Sue)* You should go to see the community charge office at the council. *(turns back)* Now, I would like to speak to Mr Gareth Jenkins. I assume he's here?

**DAN** What makes you say that?

**SAM** I rang up to check he lived here. *(crosses towards the men)*

**GARY** It must have been you your dad spoke to!

**SAM** *(beside Dan)* I take it that you are Mr Jenkins?

**DAN** Er, why do you ask officer?

**SAM** Are you Mr Jenkins

**DAN** Sorry, I can't help you.

**SAM** Sir, are you obstructing a police officer in the course of an inquiry?

**DAN** No, I'm NOT Mr Jenkins.

**SAM** Then why didn't you say so? *(turns to Gary)* Are you Mr Gareth Jenkins?

**GARY** Yes.

**SAM** Good. now we're getting somewhere! *(with a look at Dan)*

**SUE** *(sobbing quietly)* Can I go now then.

**SAM** Presently madam. Just pull yourself together. *(comes downstage centre to speak to Gary while consulting her book)* Are you the owner of a blue Cavalier Registration Number J504DCP?

**GARY** Er... No, technically speaking, I'm not.

**HAZEL** Gary what are you saying?

**SAM** Do you know who owns it?

**GARY** Yes, the Highway Leasing Company. *(tongue out at Hazel)*

**SAM** *(patiently)* Do you know who has leased it?

**GARY** My firm!

**SAM** Yes, and who drives it?

**GARY** I do ... *(getting up)* Oh God don't say I've been clamped!

**HAZEL** Gary, you haven't done something silly have you? Where have you left the car?

**GARY** It's only round the corner.

**SAM** Madam, please! If you don't mind, I'll ask the questions. Now Sir, do you mind telling me if you bought some petrol at the Crossways Garage at about 6.30 this evening?

**GARY** Well, yes I did, and I can prove it!

**SAM** That won't be necessary Sir. Did you get anything else?

**GARY** I don't think so ...

**SAM** Think carefully Sir.

*Gary looks at the ceiling.*

Did you by any chance purchase some flowers?

**GARY** Oh, yes, I did!

**SAM** Did you pay for them Sir?

**GARY** God, I forgot! They were outside on the forecourt and I put them in my case but when I went inside to pay I must have ...

**HAZEL** You silly idiot!

**SAM** Exactly! The garage videocamera recorded your every movement, and through the police computer we've traced the car to this address, and I rang up to ...

*Clive has entered from the master bedroom, the door of which had been left open so that he has heard the interrogation.*

**CLIVE** Sam! I can't get over this!

**SAM** Sir?

**CLIVE** Do you mean to say you've called here about some ... blasted bunch of flowers?

**BABS** *(entering and crossing to table)* Take it easy Clive!

**CLIVE** But it's bloody stupid! Why are you not out on the trail of some murderer or rapist?

**SAM** *(as she advances towards Clive until she is looking him in the face)* Because, Sir, those are not cases which the police require new recruits to investigate in their first week! Adultery also comes later!

*Clive is crushed again and he retreats to the table. Sue shivers a bit with the cold as Dan goes to the table and picks up the flowers to bring to Sam.*

**SAM** *(advancing)* Don't you think you ought to dress too madam?

**SUE** Yea, p'raps I better. *(goes into master bedroom)*

**DAN** Look officer. I think these must be the flowers in question. You can see they're still wrapped. I'm sure that Mr Jenkins here had simply forgotten to pay for them. Isn't that right. Gary?

**GARY** *(brightening)* Er, yes, yes that's right! Thanks Dan! *(takes the flowers from him and holds them out)* Why don't you have them officer?

**SAM** You wouldn't be trying to bribe me would you Mr Jenkins?

**GARY** Er, no, of course not... but they only cost about one fifty and I thought...

**HAZEL** Thank you very much!

**GARY** I thought that at that price ...

**SAM** The value of the article is not important Mr Jenkins!

**GARY** No?

**SAM** No, it's the principle that matters!

**GARY** Oh yes, of course it is.

**SAM** Well, since you seem to have been simply forgetful on this occasion, there will be no harm done if you get down to Crossways and pay for them. *(puts her book away)*

**GARY** Oh yes I will, first thing in the morning, or later tonight, or now if you like!

**SAM** Tomorrow will be best. The garage is shut now.

**GARY** Oh, right you are then.

**SAM** Good, see that you do. Now if you, will excuse me I'll be on my way.

**BABS** Sure you wouldn't like a nice cup of tea before you go?

**SAM** No, I wouldn't madam, thank you.

**BABS** You could have a nice chat with your dad! You've upset him.

**CLIVE** *(coming downstage right to stand beside Sam)* When I think of that expensive training and you coming round here about a miserable bunch of flowers.

**SAM** Well if you must know Sir, I rang up simply to speak to Mr Jenkins about them, but when I recognised your voice I thought I'd try a little private detective work of my own ... just for the experience you understand. Goodnight everyone!

**ALL** Goodnight, Bye Bye, G'night, Take care etc.

**SAM** Don't forget Mr Jenkins, first thing tomorrow!

**GARY** No, I won't officer ... goodnight.

*Gary gets to the door, opens it, and watches Sam walk briskly down the path. The occupants of the room react to this visit in various ways. Some sit and others exchange a quiet word until Sam has got far enough away.*

**CLIVE** Detective work was it? Official snooping if you ask me!

**DAN** *(crossing to him)* Be reasonable Clive. She has to start somewhere. She did a good job here tonight. I was quite impressed. You wouldn't really want her out chasing rapists just yet would you?

**CLIVE** Well ... no ... I suppose not.

**GARY** And she did discover other interesting things as well!

**CLIVE** Don't remind me. Samantha's always been a bit nosy.

**DAN** You ought to be proud of her! *(moves to drinks table)*

**CLIVE** Well, yes, I am, generally speaking, I suppose I am.

*Babs has come forward during the Clive-Dan interchange and now sits beside Hazel. Sue re-enters, dressed again, and goes to freshen up her drink and chat to Dan, her back to the audience.*

**BABS** I must say Hazel, your little Pete has been marvellous. Only once did he wake up for a change and a feed.

**HAZEL** Oh, yes, you weren't here when I explained were you? You see Babs, I was looking after the baby for someone else and I wanted to go out.

**GARY** *(from desk chair)* I wonder why?

**BABS** Well, any time you want me to be here, just get in touch. And I hope you WILL want my services in the future. *(gives Hazel a nudge)*

**HAZEL** You never know. So, you'll be going now then?

**BABS** Yes I think we should. Clive?

**CLIVE** *(admiring Sue's rear since her entrance)* Er, what is it old girl?

**BABS** We're off! *(getting up)*

**CLIVE** Oh, you're going are you?

**BABS** Come and take me some of the way home.

**CLIVE** Can't you get there by yourself? Remember our agreement?

**BABS** Sod our agreement - pardon my French Hazel - I've got a rotten head and the last favour I want you to do for me is help get me home!

*Clive takes a last look at Sue and reluctantly gets to his feet.*

**HAZEL** You must tell me if I owe you anything.

**BABS** Oh nothing dear. I'm sorry I didn't tell you about him. *(indicating Clive)* Apart from my hangover - no thanks to Clive - I've learned a lot. It's been a very interesting evening.

**CLIVE** *(coming forward)* Not one that I'd call very satisfying!

**GARY** You can't win them all Clive.

**HAZEL** *(rising)* Well ... I'm very grateful to you. Perhaps we'll meet up again some time.

**BABS** Yes I hope so dear.

*Hazel goes to open front door and Babs and Clive move to it.*

**BABS** Well goodnight all!

**DAN** Good night!

**SUE** G'night!

**CLIVE** Bye Gary, don't do anything I would do!

**GARY** Yeah, well.

**CLIVE** Goodnight Sue, see you at the Queen's Arms!

**SUE** 'Opefully, if I aint sacked.

**BABS** 'Bye all!

**HAZEL** Good night! Mind how you go.

*Babs and Clive have made their exit and Hazel watches them go down the path and then closes the door.*

**CLIVE** Well you were on fine form tonight!

**BABS** It's your fault. You shouldn't have drugged me. Or tried to get off with that Sue!

**CLIVE** I wouldn't have done if you'd been more entertaining.

**BABS** You ought to be ashamed of yourself! You're old enough to be her father! It wouldn't surprise me if you were!

*Meanwhile, in the living room, Gary is still moping, holding the limp flowers and Sue has continued chatting to Dan, Hazel having closed the door returns to the sofabed, tidies it, and finds Dan's script.*

**HAZEL** Here's your script Dan!

**DAN** *(coming forward to get it from Hazel)* Oh yes, mustn't go without it.

**GARY** *(mutters)* He HAS gone without it!

**DAN** Pardon?

**GARY** Nothing.

*Dan, having taken his script, is behind the sofabed. Sue comes to sit at the desk chair beside Gary.*

**DAN** *(to Hazel)* Sorry we didn't get more rehearsing done.

**HAZEL** Perhaps we should have stayed where we were. This place turned out to be even noisier. There was only Babs here when I left.

**DAN** And then people started appearing from all directions!

**GARY** What that Babs saw in Clive I can't imagine.

**SUE** You wouldn't! I thought 'e was cute.

**GARY** He was certainly cool.

**SUE** 'E wont be so cool when 'e gets 'ome!

**HAZEL** Poor Babs. I feel sorry for her.

**DAN** Yes, she seems a very genuine sort of person.

**SUE** *(after a pause)* Well, now we've got rid of 'em, why don't we 'ave a bit of a party? *(looks at Dan)*

**GARY** What with? We're practically out-of booze!

**HAZEL** And you've still got your headache.

**GARY** Oh... yeah.

**SUE** But I don't feel like going 'ome just yet. I like it 'ere.

**DAN** I do too, *(to Hazel)* but I think I'd better be off.

**GARY** *(mutters)* Been off for ages!

*Sue giggles.*

**DAN** Pardon?

**GARY** Nothing.

HAZEL I hope you don't feel the evening has been wasted Dan.
DAN Oh no, it's been ... well, different.
SUE *(to Dan)* Are you sure you gotta go?
DAN Well, I should really.
SUE 'Ow about taking me for a drink on the way?
GARY *(mutters)* Yes, you give her one Dan!

*Sue giggles.*

DAN *(to Sue)* I thought you wanted to stay a while.
SUE Yeh, but if you're goin', I better go an' all.
DAN All right then.
SUE I'll get me bag. *(downs her drink in one gulp)*
HAZEL Well, Dan I'll see you on Tuesday in the club.
GARY That's if I let you go!
HAZEL *(turns to Gary from Dan)* We've got to rehearse Gary! We've only two months and we've both got big parts.
GARY *(aside)* Well there's no answer to that.
SUE I'm ready Danny boy! I think we should 'ave our drink near the station 'cos that's where I catch me bus.
DAN Er, yes, that'll be all right.
GARY The perfect gentleman.
SUE We'll be off then. *(comes to take Dan's arm)* See you next Friday Gary?
GARY Yeah, maybe.
HAZEL *(opening door)* That's if I let YOU go!
DAN Goodnight!
SUE Ta ta.
HAZEL Goodnight! Take care!

*Hazel watches them, closes the door and back to sofabed. She and Gary sit quietly as Sue and Dan go down the path.*

SUE 'Ere Dan, I just thought of somethin'. You ain't leadin' me up the garden path, are ya? *(giggles)*
DAN Have no fear of that.
SUE *(still holding Dan's arm)* How far do you go then?
DAN How do you mean? Oh, up towards the station.
SUE That's lucky in it, same way as I 'ave to go too!
DAN My car is in the station carpark.
SUE Oooh lovely! I'll be getting 'ome in style tonight!

*When Sue and Dan have gone, Hazel and Gary, who have been looking elsewhere, catch each other's eyes, and look away again. A moment.*

HAZEL Gary?
GARY *(with Hazel)* Hazel?

**HAZEL** Sorry, go on.
**GARY** *(with Hazel)* No, after you.
**HAZEL** *(smiling)* Sorry ...
**GARY** *(with Hazel)* Sorry ...

*They look across at each other, each with an embarrassed smile.*

**HAZEL** It's my fault. I should have told you about Peter.
**GARY** Peter?
**HAZEL** The baby. Later on we shall need one for the play. When we came here I thought it would surprise Dan.
**GARY** Oh, yeah.
**HAZEL** I DID want to go to the rehearsal.
**GARY** I'm sure you did!
**HAZEL** Well, Dan has only recently joined the group and doesn't know many people. I think he's a bit lonely.
**GARY** And you wanted to give him some company! Were you the only ones rehearsing tonight?
**HAZEL** Well, yes.
**GARY** And you wanted to get to know him better?
**HAZEL** That's right.
**GARY** Did it have to be here in our home?
**HAZEL** I er, forgot my script. I'd told Babs I'd only be an hour or so. I expect she didn't hear me. Or she didn't remember.
**GARY** So you intended to bring Dan here?

*A moment. Hazel looks guilty.*

**GARY** Can't say I blame you.
**HAZEL** Well, yes. I suppose I made a mistake. *(a pause)* I'm sorry Gary. It hasn't happened before and it won't happen again.

*Pause. Gary gets up and takes her the wilting flowers at which he has been absent mindedly picking. He sits beside her holding them under her sunken head. She looks up and smiles.*

**GARY** And I don't think I should go down the Queen's Arms again. A certain barmaid may be lying in wait for me.
**HAZEL** Is that really what happened then?
**GARY** Yeah. I didn't know she had the hots for me, and, to tell you the truth, I was a bit in need of attention. She just took over.
**HAZEL** *(moving closer)* Poor Gary!
**GARY** I let slip that there was no-one here, and ...
**HAZEL** She brought you here? To have her wicked way with you?

*He nods.*

I'll have to look after you better and then you may not want to go out on your own. *(snuggles up)*

**GARY** It's dangerous out there! Harm can come to an unsuspecting young man!

**HAZEL** Unless he's protected!

**GARY** Will you protect me?

**HAZEL** Yes, of course I will, and so will this! *(holds up the condom which she has found in the sofabed)*

**GARY** Hazel, I think we should have an early night.

**HAZEL** Oh yes, why? Because of your headache?

**GARY** No, well you're not going to believe this, but, *(getting up)* first thing in the morning - oh, after I've been to the garage - second thing in the morning I'm going to dig those foundations!

**HAZEL** Well, I DO find that hard to believe!

**GARY** I think I've learnt some lessons tonight. I feel like a new man. Perhaps you did too! Did you make a pass at him?

**HAZEL** Hmm, not really. I suppose I was a bit forward.

**GARY** That's not allowed.

**HAZEL** What do you mean?

**GARY** Forward passes are not allowed ... in rugby!

**HAZEL** You and your rugby! My mild flirtation with Dan was not nearly as dangerous as Sue's. Trying to steal my man from me.

**GARY** And I'll tell you something else! I'm going to come down that drama club now and again to keep an eye on you! I may even act! Where's that script?

*Hazel's script is still on the sofabed. He sits and reaches for it.*

**HAZEL** I think you could be a good actor. You enjoy putting on voices.

**GARY** Oh, here's the bit I heard you and Dan doing! *(reads putting on an assumed manner)* "Yes I know that if I'm found guilty I may be separated from you for years but that's better than to keep meeting you for a few stolen moments while I'm on the run."

**HAZEL** "Oh darling, darling! When shall I see you again?"

**GARY** "Why did this have to happen to us?"

**HAZEL** "Hold me close, swear that you love me!"

**GARY** I bloody well love you!

*They laugh and cuddle.*

**HAZEL** Gary, you know what I think we should do now?

**GARY** Tell me, tell me, tell me.

**HAZEL** I also think we should have an early night! I know a good cure for headaches!

**GARY** Well, you know what I think, my Hazelnut?

**HAZEL** Tell me, tell me, tell me.

**GARY** That we won't need this! *(takes the condom from her and goes to the waste paper basket, picks up the ball and drops condom in)*

**HAZEL** What are you saying?

**GARY** I'm saying, Hazel, that you and I, should go in there, and make our own baby!

**HAZEL** Oh Gary! *(rises)* Can we afford it?

**GARY** We shall have to afford it!

*Hazel flings her arms round him, trapping the ball between them.*

**GARY** I also think I should get rid of this! *(opens the door and boots the ball deep into the garden, watching it go)* And this! *(takes off his old rugby shirt and dumps it in the wheely bin, then closes the door)*

**HAZEL** Come on then! *(moves to bedroom)* When we get to bed, you won't call me Sue will you?

**GARY** And you won't go calling me Dan?

**HAZEL** Oh, I don't know about that! *(laughs as she exits)*

**GARY** *(stretches his arms and legs, mutters "God what an evening!" and he swaggers to the lightswitch and is about to turn it off when he hears the cry of the baby)* Leave this to me Hazel! *(crosses the stage and enters the spare room as there is a second cry from the baby. Then, off)* There's a good chap! Everything's all right! *(enters with the baby in his arms and starts slowly walking round the room)* Now, what's the matter with you little man? You've been fed and watered? And you're still very sleepy aren't you? I'm sure that there's nothing to worry about. You just close your eyes again cos Gary's got some other kind of cuddling to do. *(He has slowly crossed the stage and turned towards the bathroom where he sees the picture of the rugby player on the door. He bows to it and his pace quickens as he moves the baby to hold it like a rugby ball and his voice takes on again the tones of the rugby commentator)* And another brilliant pass from the pack finds Rory Underwood in the clear within yards of the Welsh line! He strikes out for what proves to be the final touchdown of the game ...

**HAZEL** *(emerging in her underwear from the bedroom as Gary has reached the front door)* Gary?

**GARY** *(coming to a halt and turning sheepishly towards her)* Yes dear?

**HAZEL** Oh ... Nothing!

*They look at each other happily as the curtain quickly falls.*

===

## LIGHTING AND EFFECTS PLOT

### ACT 1

| Cue 1 | Whistling kettle | Page 1 |
| Cue 2 | TV turned off | Page 2 |
| Cue 3 | Gary "... the Queen's Arms." Telephone rings | Page 6 |
| Cue 4 | Gary at rear of auditorium Sounds of gate, cat, car? | Page 7 |
| Cue 5 | Babs "... I didn't mean it." Telephone rings - stop 3 lines later | Page 12 |
| Cue 6 | Clive "... receive boarders!" Lights are dimmed | Page 14 |
| Cue 7 | Gary "...What would you like?" Lights brighter | Page 15 |
| Cue 8 | Gary "... Let's see... what's this?" Cassette plays | Page 18 |
| Cue 9 | Gary "a haka, listen" | Page 18 |
| Cue 10 | Gary "Get her out" Toilet flushes | Page 22 |
| Cue 11 | Sue "...Oh, about a year I suppose" Telephone rings | Page 29 |
| Cue 12 | Clive "... Right then, enter!" Lights are dimmed | Page 31 |
| Cue 13 | Sue ". . . Get down 'ere!" Cries of baby | Page 32 |

### ACT 2

| Cue 14 | Lights up | Page 33 |
| Cue 15 | Gary "you know where it is" Loud click of gate | Page 38 |
| Cue 16 | Hazel "...First heard this when I was" Cassette switched on, then off | Page 41 |
| Cue 17 | Hazel "tart into the house?" Doorbell rings | Page 53 |
| Cue 18 | Sam "... So I've been told, thank you madam." Toilet flushes | Page 55 |
| Cue 19 | Gary's offstage cry " God what an evening" Baby's cry | Page 64 |

## FURNITURE AND PROPERTY LIST

**On stage.**

Welsh dresser with various dishes.

Dining table. On it: cans and glasses, cruets including sauce, remains of fish and chip supper.

Drinks table. On it: glasses and variety of drinks including Cinzano, brandy, vodka, ginger ale.

Wall unit. On it: books video tapes, cassette recorder, audio tapes, Hazel's script of 'On the Run', ashtray, small television and VTR.

Sofabed. On it: Gary's tie, cushions.

On Chair by TV Unit: Gary's jacket containing money. Three other upright chairs

Two small tables one either side of sofabed Thick rug.

Beanbag.

Waste paper basket.

Writing desk. On it: photos of drama group (also on wall), a wedding photo, rugby trophy.

Small table down stage. On it: telephone. Beside it: briefcase in which there is a bunch of flowers.

An old rugby ball in a suitable cupboard (e.g.under drinks) On bathroom door: Poster of Rory Underwood Other ornaments, plants, radiators as appropriate

**In Master Bedroom:**

Hazel's handbag. In it: cassette, lipstick, doorkey, Hazel's jacket.

Gary's old rugby jersey, jeans and trainers, lady's dressing gown.

Condom.

Blanket or rug rolled into a ball.

**In Bathroom:**

Mirror on wall, towel rail.

**In Kitchen:**

Variety of crisps, coffee mugs, rolling pin, milk bottle, fresh air spray.

**In Spareroom.**

Doll as baby, nappies and baby's bottle.

**Outside front door:**

Steps leading down into garden.

Beside steps: wheely bin, milk bottle container, garden bench

**Personal:**

Babs: handbag.
Sue: handbag.
Clive: cigarettes & lighter Dan: script, pencil torch.
Sam: police notebook & pencil.

**THE SET**

Backing

Mirror  Bathroom  Kitchen
hatch
Dresser  Table
Drinks table  to Kitchen

to Master bedroom  Sofabed  Plant
Rug  To Spare bedroom
Large unit  Desk
Beanbag
Basket
Telephone
Window  Door  Window
Wheely bin  Steps  Garden bench